Fodor's
25 Best

MUNICH

How to Use
This Book

This guide is divided into four sections

• Essential Munich: An introduction to the city and tips on making the most of your stay.

• Munich by Area: We've broken the city into five areas, and recommended the best sights, shops, entertainment venues, nightlife and restaurants in each one. Suggested walks help you to explore on foot.

• Where to Stay: The best hotels, whether you're looking for luxury, budget or something in between.

• Need to Know: The info you need to make your trip run smoothly, including getting about by public transport, weather tips, emergency phone numbers and useful websites.

Navigation In the Munich by Area chapter, we've given each area its own color, which is also used on the locator maps throughout the book and the map on the inside front cover.

Maps The fold-out map accompanying this book is a comprehensive street plan of Munich. The grid on this fold-out map is the same as the grid on the locator maps within the book. We've given grid references within the book for each sight and listing.

Contents

Introducing Munich

Think Munich, think Oktoberfest, BMWs and lederhosen! But there's so more to the Bavarian capital. Its unique atmosphere is hard to define but many have tried: village of a million; metropolis with a heart; the secret capital of Germany.

With its big-city atmosphere, rural Alpine charm, art treasures, folk customs and high-tech industry, this cosmopolitan yet traditional metropolis manages to combine German urban efficiency with Southern European *savoir vivre*. According to a national survey, over half the German population, given the choice, would like to live here. As author Thomas Wolfe once remarked: "How can one speak of Munich but to say it is a kind of German heaven? Some people sleep and dream they are in paradise, but all over Germany people dream they have gone to Munich."

The city's close historic associations with the rise of Nazism cannot be ignored. However, we can be grateful that after World War II, although half its buildings were reduced to rubble, unlike so many German cities, Munich chose to restore and reconstruct the great palaces and churches of its past.

Many visitors are attracted to its handsome parks and palaces, its world-class museums, galleries and opera house. Others are drawn by the patriotism and deep-rooted conservatism of its inhabitants who still cherish their age-old folk traditions. For lederhosen and felt hats with shaving-brush tufts are de rigueur here, not to mention the busty dirndl-clad waitresses in the beer cellars clasping at least a dozen steins of lager. And, as you link arms with a stranger to sway to the music of an oom-pah band in one of the city's celebrated beer gardens, the atmosphere brings out the best in everyone: an infectious sociability, a passion for outdoor life and, above all, the Münchners' *joie de vivre*.

Facts + Figures

- Munich hosts the world's largest beer festival and is home to six breweries.
- Munich has 1,200km of cycle paths and bikes represent 17 percent of the traffic.
- Bayern Munich is Germany's most successful football club with 24 league titles, 17 cup victories and 8 European trophies.

MUNICH AND NAZISM

Munich will always be associated with Adolf Hitler. Indeed, he once remarked "Munich is the city closest to my heart. Here as a young man, as a soldier and as a politician I made my start." It was here, at the famous bloody Beer Hall Putsch of 1923 when he stormed a meeting of local dignitaries in the Bürgerbräukeller, that he made his first bid for power.

MYSTERY WIND

The famous föhn wind, Munich's unique weather phenomenon, can strike at any time of year. This warm, dry Alpine wind guarantees blue skies and crystal-clear views (the Alps seem close enough to touch) but it is also blamed for head-aches and bad moods. So if barmaids seem more short-tempered and the locals blunter than usual, perhaps it's the föhn!

MANN'S SHINING CITY

"München leuchtet" (Munich shone), the opening words of *Gladius Dei* (1902) by the celebrated German writer and Nobel Prize winner Thomas Mann, is without doubt one of Munich's most famous quotations. Today, Munich remains Mann's shining city. His words are on its medal of honor—"Munich shines—on Munich's friends."

A Short Stay in Munich

DAY 1

Morning Start the day with a traditional Bavarian breakfast of *Weisswürste* (boiled white sausages) at the **Weisses Bräuhaus** (▷ 42). A true Münchner enjoys them with a stein of beer!

Mid-morning Make your way to **Marienplatz** (▷ 28) in the Altstadt (old town). This is where the city's heart beats loudest. The square is dominated by its neo-Gothic town hall. Watch its Glockenspiel in action at 11am or midday, then climb 306 steps up the tower of nearby **Peterskirche** (▷ 31) for a brilliant view of the city.

Lunch Taste some local delicacies from various stands at the **Viktualienmarkt** (▷ 33), known for its vibrant market traders.

Afternoon Head to the **Kunstareal** ("art district") where you can experience a remarkable two millennia of Western art in just a handful of museums and galleries.

Mid-afternoon Choose from the **Staatliche Antikensammlung** or the **Glyptothek** (▷ 67) for classical treasures; the **Alte Pinakothek** (▷ 63) for Old Master paintings; the **Neue Pinakothek** (▷ 69) for medieval to Impressionist art, and the **Pinakothek der Moderne** (▷ 70) for 20th- to 21st-century collections.

Dinner Return to the heart of the city for a substantial Bavarian meal in **Haxnbauer** (▷ 58), an atmospheric old inn where chefs cook giant shanks of pork *(Schweinshax'n)* over open beechwood fires.

Evening Where better to spend your first evening in Munich than soaking up the atmosphere in the legendary **Hofbräuhaus** (▷ 47).

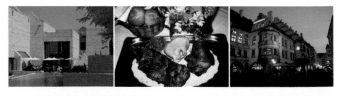

DAY 2

Morning All the family will love the world-famous **Deutsches Museum** (▷ 24) with its fascinating hands-on science exhibits.

Mid-morning Shopaholics should enjoy souvenir shopping in the pedestrianized heart of the city. **Kaufingerstrasse** is the main shopping precinct, while **Theatinerstrasse** and **Maximilianstrasse** contain the city's most exclusive boutiques.

Lunch The tiny **Nürnberger Bratwurst Glöckl** (▷ 42) is popular with both locals and tourists alike, with its warm, friendly atmosphere and some of the best sausages in Munich, grilled over an open fire and served with mountains of sauerkraut on pewter plates.

Afternoon Head west to visit **Schloss Nymphenburg** (▷ 81), summer residence of the Wittelsbachs, and to stroll in its magnificent grounds; or relax in the **Englischer Garten** (▷ 64), Munich's famous green lung, where locals go walking, jogging, busking, swimming and sunbathing.

Mid-afternoon Enjoy some refreshment at the **Chinesischer Turm** (▷ 65) beer garden, one of Germany's largest beer gardens, seating 7,000 people.

Dinner Tuck into some traditional Bavarian fare at **Spatenhaus** (▷ 58), before crossing Max-Weber-Platz for an evening's operatic entertainment at the celebrated **Nationaltheater** (▷ 48, 57). If opera is not your style, there's sophisticated **Schumann's** (▷ 57) for cocktails.

Evening Party animals will find plenty of late-night bars and clubs in the **Gärtnerplatz** district, or head to trendy **Schwabing** to see and be seen.

Top 25

►►►

These pages are a quick guide to the Top 25, which are described in more detail later. Here they are listed alphabetically, and the tinted background shows which area they are in.

Bayerisches National-museum ▷ 46 A taste of Bavarian life over the centuries.

BMW Museum ▷ 86 This dazzling museum provides a fascinating display of transport technology.

Dachau ▷ 98–99 A pretty town that is infamous as the site of the first Nazi concentration camp.

Deutsches Museum ▷ 24–25 One of the largest and best science museums in the world.

Englischer Garten ▷ 64–65 Popular for walking, cycling, sunbathing or relaxing in a beer garden.

Frauenkirche ▷ 27 The twin onion-shape domes are a symbol of Munich.

Hofbräuhaus ▷ 47 The world's most famous pub, a Munich institution.

Jüdisches Museum ▷ 32 Purpose-built cultural center and small but engaging museum serving Munich's growing Jewish community.

Königsplatz ▷ 66–67 This "Athens-on-the-Isar" is a majestic square with three neoclassical temples.

Lenbachhaus ▷ 68 A delightful gallery of 19th- and 20th-century art housed in an Italianate villa.

Nationaltheater ▷ 48 Restored to its pre-war glory and home to the Bavarian State Opera.

Münchner Stadtmuseum ▷ 30 The city's vibrant history from medieval times to the present day.

Marienplatz and Neues Rathaus ▷ 28–29 The city's main square, a great place to people-watch.

Map labels:
RIESENFELD
ALTE HEIDE
BMW Museum
Petuelpark
Nordfriedhof
Luitpoldpark
Hasenbergl
WEST SCHWABING
MAXVORSTADT & SCHWABING 59–78
SCHWABING
Leopoldpark
Englischer Garten
Isar
Neue Pinakothek
Alte Pinakothek
Lenbachhaus
Pinakothek der Moderne
Alter Nordlicher Friedhof
Königsplatz
Odeonsplatz
Hofgarten
Alter Botanical Garten
Residenz
National-theater
INNENSTADT NORD 43–58
BOGENHAUSEN
LUDWIGS-VORST
Frauenkirche
Neues Rathaus
Marienplatz
Hofbräuhaus
Bayerisches Nationalmuseum
Maximilian anlagen
Asamkirche
Peterskirche
Viktualienmarkt
STEIN-HAUSEN
Jüdisches Museum
Münchner Stadtmuseum
Deutsches Museum
HAIDHAUSEN
Alter Süd friedhof
ISARVORST
Frühlings-an Lagen
INNENSTADT SÜD 20–42
Ostfriedhof

Shopping

Munich's most popular shopping street is without doubt the pedestrian zone between Karlsplatz and Marienplatz—one kilometer (half a mile) of shopping fun with huge department stores interspersed with boutiques and grocery stores. Even when the shops are closed this area is packed with window-shoppers. German fashions, leather and sportswear are all good buys. Just off Marienplatz, sports fans will revel in the giant sports department stores of Schuster and Sportscheck (▷ 39), where you can buy everything from golf tees to skiing holidays.

Munich Fashion

Munich is the capital of Germany's fashion industry, and you will be amazed at the city's enormous range of boutiques from haute couture and Bavarian *Trachten* (folk costume) to wacky new trends. In the elegant shops of Theatiner-strasse, Residenzstrasse and Maximilianstrasse famous designer labels rub shoulders with the classic Munich boutique of Bogner (▷ 55).

Waterproof cloth

Be sure to visit Loden-Frey (▷ 56), the largest shop for national costumes in the world—look for articles in Loden cloth, a Bavarian specialty. This waterproof wool fabric, in grey, navy or traditional green, has kept Münchners warm in winter for generations.

CULINARY DELIGHTS

Local culinary specialties include countless types of tasty sausage, best eaten with *Süßsenf* (sweet mustard), as well as aromatic regional herbs and fine breads and cheese, all magnificently displayed on green wooden stalls at the traditional open-air Viktualienmarkt (▷ 33), while Dallmayr (▷ 55) and Feinkost Käfer (▷ 55) are among the finest delicatessens in Europe. For truly unique chocolates, visit Elly Seidl (▷ 55), famous for its *Münchner Küppeln* chocolates, shaped like the onion-domes of the Frauenkirche.

Tulips on Neuhauserstrasse (top left); a Nutcracker doll stall at the Christmas Market (middle)

Shopping in Maximiliansplatz (top right); Munich's open-air Viktualienmarkt (above)

Publishing and Porcelain

As one of the world's leading publishing cities, with over 3,000 publishing houses, it is hardly surprising that Munich boasts a wide variety of bookshops, concentrated in the city's core and near the university in Schellingstrasse. Antiques shops, too, are popular, with many specializing in "English," Jugendstil (art nouveau) and art deco styles. Collectors keep a look out for old Meissen or modern Rosenthal, while the famous Nymphenburg porcelain (▷ 56, 90)—produced in Munich since 1747—is still manufactured in its traditional rococo designs. For the finest in Bavarian handicrafts, visit the Kunstgewerbeverein (▷ 56) in Pacellistrasse, or the numerous streets converging on Max-Joseph-Platz, for unique Bavarian gifts, including handmade puppets, carnival masks and porcelain beer steins.

Beer and Breweries

No shopping spree would be complete without purchasing some of Munich's beer. The main breweries are Spaten-Franziskaner, Augustiner, Löwenbräu, Hacker-Pschorr, Hofbräuhaus and Paulaner. There are special glasses for special beers, special beers for certain seasons. And with beer halls everywhere, it won't take long to find out if you prefer *dunkles*, *Weissbier*, *Pils* or *helles*… As they say in Munich, *Prost*!

SPECIALTY SHOPPING

Munich has a large number of small, old-fashioned shops that concentrate on one or two articles—for example, musical boxes, felt, buttons, knives, wood-carvings and even lederhosen—and which are still to be found in the middle of town. Some of the best buys in Munich include German-made binoculars, telescopes, kitchenware, electronic gadgets and bed linen. The presence of so many top orchestras in Germany results in top-notch musical instruments. Germany is also known for its manufacture of children's toys. You'll find everything from train sets and teddy bears to traditional dolls and handmade puppets.

Shopping by Theme

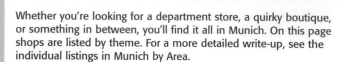

Whether you're looking for a department store, a quirky boutique, or something in between, you'll find it all in Munich. On this page shops are listed by theme. For a more detailed write-up, see the individual listings in Munich by Area.

ANTIQUES

Antike Uhren Eder
   (▷ 55)
Landpartie (▷ 74)

BOOKS

Deutsches Museum Shop
   (▷ 38)
Hugendubel (▷ 38)
Words' Worth (▷ 74)

CHILDREN

Kinder-Ambiente (▷ 74)
Kunst und Spiel (▷ 74)
Obletter (▷ 39)
Die Puppenstube (▷ 74)

DEPARTMENT STORES

Galeria Kaufhof (▷ 38)
Karstadt (▷ 38, 90)
Ludwig Beck (▷ 39)
Olympia Einkaufszentrum
   (OEZ)(▷ 90)
Sportscheck (▷ 39)

FASHION

Behringer (▷ 55)
Bogner (▷ 55)
Bree (▷ 55)
Bube & Dame (▷ 90)
Eduard Meier (▷ 55)
Flip (▷ 74)
Fourth Dimension
   (▷ 38)
Hallhuber (▷ 74)
Hemmerle (▷ 56)
Hirmer (▷ 38)
Konen (▷ 38)

Lederhosen Wagner
   (▷ 39)
Loden-Frey (▷ 56)
Theresa (▷ 56)

FOOD AND MARKETS

L'Antipasto (▷ 90)
Armin's Räucherkuchl
   (▷ 90)
Boettner (▷ 55)
Le Chalet du Fromage
   (▷ 74)
Dallmayr (▷ 55)
Eilles (▷ 55, 90)
Elisabethmarkt (▷ 74)
Elly Seidl (▷ 55)
Espresso & Barista
   (▷ 90)
Feinkost Käfer (▷ 55)
Markt am Wiener Platz
   (▷ 56)
Rischart (▷ 39)
Schmidt (▷ 39)
Spanisches Fruchthaus
   (▷ 39)
Viktualienmarkt
   (▷ 33, 39)

GIFTS AND BAVARIAN SOUVENIRS

Angermaier (▷ 90)
Butlers (▷ 55)
Geschenke Kaiser
   (▷ 38)
Holz Leute (▷ 38)
Kunstgewerbeverein
   (▷ 56)
Max Krug (▷ 39)
Porzellanmanufaktur
   Nymphenburg
   (▷ 56, 90)

Stockhammer (▷ 74)
Weihnachtsmarkt
   (▷ panel 39, 90)

INTERIOR DESIGN AND ART

2-Rad (▷ 74)
Deco Susanne Klein
   (▷ 38)
Hussfeld und Zang
   (▷ 90)
Kaut-Bullinger (▷ 38)
Kokon (▷ 56)
Kremer Pigmente (▷ 74)
Kristina Sack (▷ 90)
Schreibmayr (▷ 56)

SPECIALIST SHOPS

China's World (▷ 74)
Dehner (▷ 38)
Fanshop (▷ 55)
Ludwig Beck Beauty
   (▷ 56)
Messer & Scheren
   (▷ 39)
Perlenmarkt (▷ 74)
Rosenthal (▷ 56)

Munich by Night

Munich's nightlife is relatively small-scale and provincial compared to some cities. On a mild summer's evening, nothing beats strolling through the old town, seeing the illuminated historic buildings, or pausing to enjoy a drink or an ice cream on the broad sidewalk terraces of Leopoldstrasse.

Eating and Drinking

Eating and drinking in Munich are major pastimes, with options ranging from hearty Bavarian fare washed down with massive liter-steins of beer in the local Bierkellers to some of Germany's finest restaurants. In both beer cellars and beer gardens, it is normal to sit together with other guests at long communal tables.

City of Music

Munich is a city of music, with a famous opera-house long associated with Mozart, Wagner and Richard Strauss, and three major symphony orchestras. The *Münchner Festspiele* festival in July and August marks the musical highpoint of the year, attracting top international singers and opera aficionados. There's always something musical happening, from choral works and organ recitals in churches, open-air concerts in royal palaces, to live jazz, blues and rock venues, not to mention marionette-opera performances and even yodeling. If your German is good enough, Munich also offers a dazzling schedule of first-rate theater, ranging from classical and contemporary productions to political cabaret.

NIGHT SPOTS

Early-closing laws prevent many places from staying open all night, but Munich has plenty of vibrant bars and clubs, many on Gärtnerplatz, the student district of Schwabing and the Glockenbach quarter. Choose from foaming beer steins and drunken swaying to the oom-pah bands of the beer halls or sophisticated cocktails in Germany's trendiest nightspots.

Fun and beer-drinking at the Oktoberfest (top and middle); Cuvilliés-Theater in the Residenz (above)

Eating Out

Bavarian food, usually accompanied by a beer, is hearty and heavy and is almost always based on meat. White sausages, dumplings, sauerkraut and roast pork are just a few examples of local cuisine. Beer halls *(Brauhäuser)* are the best places to try traditional German food and sample some of the city's own beers.

Italian Connection

Munich has a strong affinity with Italy, which means the city has plenty of Italian restaurants. Locals share the Italians' love of dining alfresco —at the first hint of sunshine, chairs and tables are swiftly moved outside to terraces, court-yards and gardens. In recent years, the number of Thai, Japanese, Mexican and tapas restaurants in the city has also grown.

When to Eat

In Munich, people like to eat early and it is not unusual to find older Munich residents having lunch as early as 11.15am. As hotel breakfast buffets are substantial, you may not be hungry enough for an early lunch. In this case, choose one of the many bars, cafés and restaurants that serve full meals or even breakfast right into the afternoon. In the evening, those restaurants that aren't open all day start serving at about 6pm. Non-smokers will likely be pleased to learn that smoking is banned in bars, cafés and restaurants except in separate rooms (where these exist).

BÄCKEREIEN AND *KAFFEE UND KUCHEN*

Bakeries (*Bäckereien*) are usually the first eateries to open in the morning. They serve an overwhelming array of cakes, pastries, breads and coffees at very reasonable prices. Many bakeries have a small seating or stand-ing area, so you can eat your purchases there. Cafés in Germany also often open as early as 7 or 8am, and tend to serve a wide range of light snacks, in addition to *Kaffee und Kuchen* (coffee and cakes), which are usually enjoyed mid-morning or late in the afternoon.

Top to bottom: Café Glockenspiel; a Munich beer garden; a street café in Neumarkt; traditional Würste

Restaurants by Cuisine

There are restaurants to suit all tastes and budgets in Munich. On this page they are listed by cuisine. For a more detailed description of each restaurant, see Munich by Area.

AFTERNOON TEA

Kempinski Hotel Vier Jahreszeiten (▷ 58)
Schlosscafé im Palmenhaus (▷ 92)

BAVARIAN CUISINE

Augustiner Gaststätten (▷ 41)
Bachmaier Hofbräu (▷ 77)
Hacker-Pschorr Bräuhaus (▷ 92)
Halali (▷ 58)
Haxnbauer im Scholastikahaus (▷ 58)
Hofbräuhaus (▷ 47)
Löwenbräukeller (▷ 92)
Nürnberger Bratwurst Glöckl (▷ 42)
Ratskeller (▷ 42)
Schlemmermeyer (▷ 42)
Spatenhaus an der Oper (▷ 58)
Spezlwirtschaft (▷ 42)
Weisses Bräuhaus (▷ 42)
Zum Alten Markt (▷ 42)

BEER GARDENS

Augustiner-Keller (▷ 92)
Hirschgarten (▷ 92)
Kloster Andechs (▷ 102)
Max Emanuel Bräuerei (▷ 77)

Seehaus im Englischen Garten (▷ 78)
Taxisgarten (▷ 92)
Waldwirtschaft Grosshesselohe (▷ 102)
Zum Flaucher (▷ 102)
Zur Schwaige (▷ 92)

CAFÉS

Café Altschwabing (▷ 77)
Café Frischhut (▷ 41)
Café Glockenspiel (▷ 41)
Café Haidhausen (▷ 41)
Café Reitschule (▷ 77)
Café Wiener Platz (▷ 58)
Eisbach (▷ 58)
News Bar (▷ 78)
Schelling-Salon (▷ 78)
Tresznjewski (▷ 78)

GOURMET

Bogenhauser Hof (▷ 58)
Huckebein Essen & Wein (▷ 77)
Käfer-Schänke (▷ 58)
Königshof (▷ 41)
Rilano No. 6 (▷ 78)
Rue des Halles (▷ 42)
Tantris (▷ 78)

ICE CREAM

Adamello (▷ 41)
Sarcletti (▷ 92)

INTERNATIONAL CUISINE

Le Cézanne (▷ 77)
Joe Peña's (▷ 41)
Maredo (▷ 41)
Master's Home (▷ 41)
Oskar Maria im Literaturhaus (▷ 58)
Osteria (▷ 78)
Romans (▷ 92)
Rosso Pizza (▷ 78)
Sausalito's (▷ 78)
Seoul (▷ 78)
La Stella (▷ 78)
Tiramisu (▷ 78)
Trader Vic's (▷ 58)
Vinaiolo (▷ 42)

SNACKS

Münchner Suppenküche (▷ 42)
Nordsee (▷ 41)
Vincenz Murr (▷ 42)
Vini e Panini (▷ 78)

VEGETARIAN

Café Ignaz (▷ 77)
Café Ruffini (▷ 92)
Prinz Myshkin (▷ 42)

Top Tips For...

However you'd like to spend your time in Munich, these top suggestions should help you tailor your ideal visit. Each sight or listing has a fuller write-up elsewhere in the book.

EXPLORING ON A SHOE-STRING

Visit Munich's churches for free, including lofty Frauenkirche (▷ 27), sumptuous Asamkirche (▷ 26) and beautiful Theatinerkirche (▷ 49).
Window-shop on glamorous Maximilianstrasse, with its glitzy designer boutiques.
Climb the Olympiaturm (▷ 82–83) for spectacular views of the city and its Alpine backdrop.
While away an afternoon people-watching in the Englischer Garten (▷ 64–65).

CHILDREN'S ACTIVITIES

Star in a movie at the Bavaria Filmstadt (▷ 96–97).
Enjoy a dazzling performance at Munich's internationally acclaimed Circus Krone (▷ 91).
Marvel at science at the Deutsches Museum (▷ 24–25).
Visit the world's first Geo-Zoo (▷ 102).

The Olympic Tower; the 4-D Cinema Experience at the Filmstadt (above)

STAYING IN LUXURY

Check into Munich's top hotel, the Kempinski Vier Jahreszeiten (▷ 112).
Be pampered at Le Meridien's luxurious spa (▷ 112).
Enjoy the top-notch restaurant at the majestic Königshof hotel (▷ 112).
Cosset yourself in the stylish surroundings of boutique hotel Ritzi (▷ 112).

LOCAL DELICACIES

Order the best *Weisswürste* in town at the Weisses Bräuhaus (▷ 42).
Try some Leberkäs (meat loaf), or *Bratwurst* with sweet mustard, from one of the stands at the Viktualienmarkt (▷ 33).
Tuck into a gigantic pork shank (*Schweinshax'n*) at Haxnbauer (▷ 58).

Spa pampering (above right); a traditional meal of beer and sausages (right)

An evening of jazz; enjoying a stein of beer (below)

LIVE MUSIC

Chill out at the city's celebrated Jazzclub Unterfahrt (▷ 57).

Enjoy an evening of yodeling at the tiny Jodlerwirt (▷ 57)—there's nothing more Bavarian.

Assess the future of German classical music at a concert or recital in the Hochschule für musik (▷ 72).

DRINKING BEER

Try the Bavarian beer at the legendary Hofbräuhaus (▷ 47).

See and be seen at Hirschgarten beer garden (▷ 92).

Relax at the Chinesischer Turm beer garden in the Englischer Garten (▷ 64–65).

Enjoy live jazz at the atmospheric Grosshesselohe beer garden (▷ 102).

CONTEMPORARY ARCHITECTURE

Tour the new, space-age Allianz Arena football stadium (▷ 101).

Notice how BMW's towering HQ (▷ 87) resembles a four-leaf clover.

See a symbol of modern Munich: Olympiapark's futuristic tent-roof (▷ 82).

Visit the 21st-century Herz-Jesu-Kirche (▷ 87), which boasts the world's largest church doors.

Herz-Jesu-Kirche (above)

SHOPPING FOR BAVARIAN SOUVENIRS

Try on some Trachten (Bavarian folk costume) at Loden-Frey (▷ 56).

Taste glühwein and gingerbread while shopping at the annual *Weihnachtsmarkt* on Marienplatz (▷ panel, 39).

Shop for the fine pewter ornaments that make unusual and attractive gifts at Geschenke Kaiser (▷ 38).

The Weihnachtsmarkt (Christmas Market, left)

BIRD'S-EYE CITY VIEWS

Frauenkirche; freshly squeezed juices (below)

Dine in the revolving restaurant atop the Olympiaturm (▷ 82–83), with its breathtaking views of the city and the Alps.

Climb the steps of Peterskirche's tower (▷ 31) for the best bird's-eye views of the city.

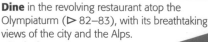

Look down on Marienplatz from the Neues Rathaus (▷ 28–29) viewing tower.

Climb one of the celebrated onion domes atop the Frauenkirche (▷ 27) for 360-degree views of the city.

EATING BRUNCH

Join the beautiful people for eggs Benedict and freshly squeezed juices at Eisbach (▷ 58).

Enjoy a sunny breakfast on the terrace of Cafe Reitschule (▷ 77).

Try trendy Café Altschwabing for a traditional Bavarian brunch (▷ 77).

HIP BARS

Rub shoulders with models and celebrities at Schumann's (▷ 57), Munich's most sophisticated bar.

Take your pick at sleek P1 (▷ 57), which offers Munich's beautiful people a choice of eight bars to suit all tastes and moods.

Swap chic for rock at Schwabinger Podium (▷ 76).

Enjoy exotic cocktails at Master's Home (▷ 40), a long-standing favorite with Münchners.

Cocktails (above); Peterskirche and the maypole (below)

BEAUTIFUL CHURCHES

Marvel at the lavish interior and religious treasures of the Asamkirche (▷ 26).

Admire the lofty Michaelskirche (▷ 35), the largest Renaissance church north of the Alps.

Hear the bells chime at Peterskirche (▷ 31), the city's oldest parish church.

Seek out the Devil's footprint inside Munich's Frauenkirche cathedral (▷ 27).

Munich by Area

INNENSTADT SÜD

INNENSTADT NORD

MAXVORSTADT AND SCHWABING

WEST MUNICH

FARTHER AFIELD

The city center is where Munich's heart beats loudest. From Marienplatz, the main square, it's just a stone's throw to the city's cathedral, the robust daily market and the main pedestrian shopping precinct.

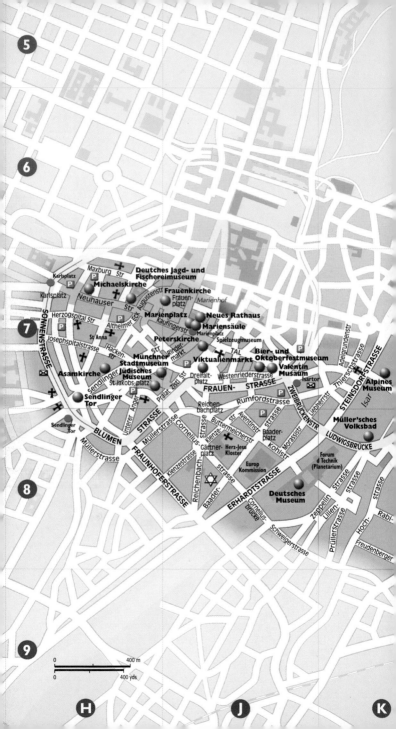

5

6

7

8

9

Maxburg Str
Karlsplatz
P
**Deutches Jagd- und
Fischereimuseum**
Michaelskirche
Augustenstr
Karlsplatz
Frauenkirche
Neuhauser Str
Frauen-
platz
Marienhof
Herzogspital str
P
Altheimer Eck
Marienplatz
Neues Rathaus
St Anna
Kaufingerstr
Mariensäule
Josephspitalstrasse
Hacken-
str
Peterskirche
Spielzeugmuseum
Marienplatz
SONNENSTRASSE
Str
Rinder-
markt
**Münchner
Stadtmuseum**
TAL
**Bier- und
Oktoberfestmuseum**
P
Adelgrundenstr
Asamkirche
Sendlinger
**Jüdisches
Museum**
St Jakobs-platz
Viktualienmarkt
**Valentin
Museum**
Isartor
STEINSDORFSTRASSE
**Alpines
Museum**
Dreifalt-
platz
Westenriederstrasse
Thierschstrasse
Isar
**Sendlinger
Tor**
P
Prälat zistl str
FRAUEN- STRASSE
Liebherrstr
ZWEIBRÜCKENSTR
Sendlinger
Tor
Anger
Reichenbach-
str
Rumfordstrasse
**Müller'sches
Volksbad**
BLUMEN
STRASSE
Müllerstrasse
Cornelius-
strasse
Aventinstr
P
Baader-
platz
Moraßistr
Kohlstr
LUDWIGSBRÜCKE
Müllerstrasse
Kenze-
str
Buttermelcherstr
strasse
FRAUNHOFERSTRASSE
Kienzestrasse
Reichenbach-
strasse
gärtner-
platz
**Herz-Jesu
Kloster**
**Europ
Kommission**
strasse
d Technik
(Planetarium)
Forum
Zeppelin
strasse
Baader-
ERHARDTSTRASSE
Cornelius-
brücke
**Deutsches
Museum**
Lilien-
strasse
Hoch-
strasse
schweigerstrasse
Prüllerstrasse
Rabl-
strasse
Freudenberger

0   400 m
0   400 yds

H   **J**   **K**

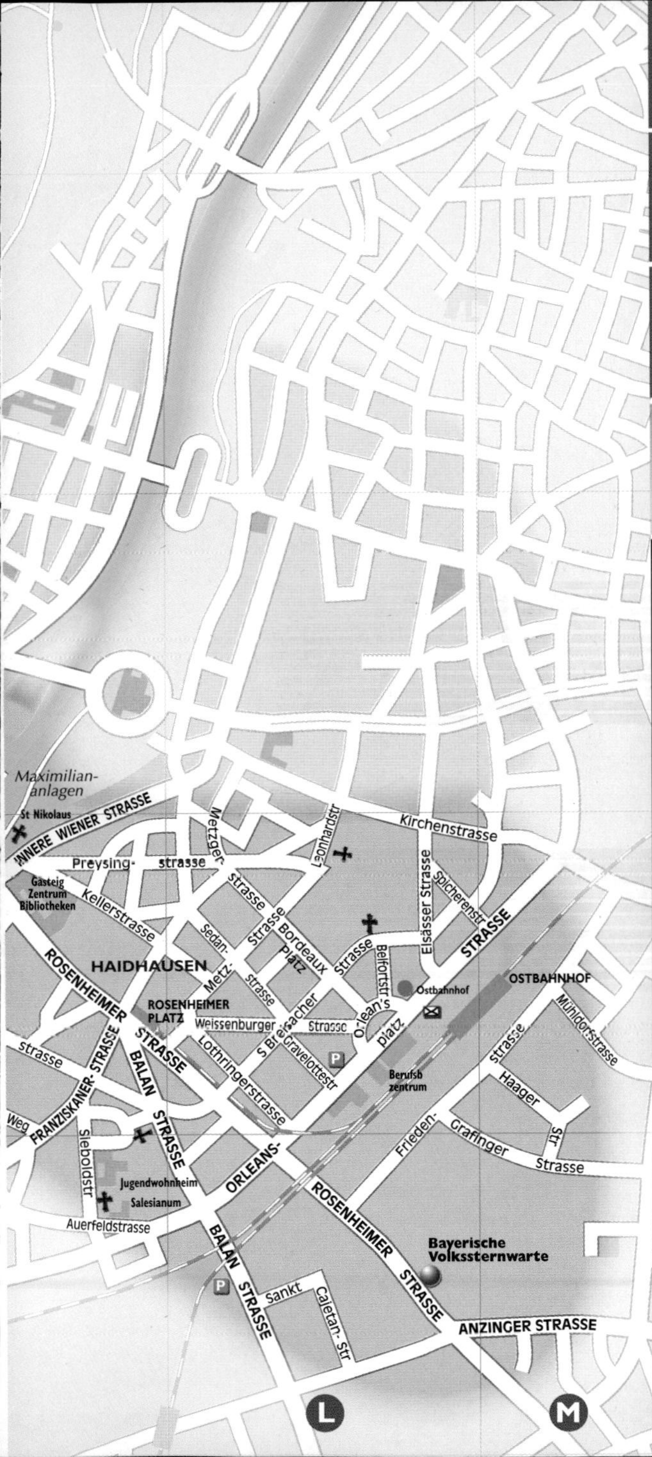

Maximilian-
anlagen

St Nikolaus

INNERE WIENER STRASSE

Preysing-
strasse

Kirchenstrasse

Metzger-
strasse

Leonhardstr

Gasteig
Zentrum
Bibliotheken

Kellerstrasse

Elsasser Strasse

Sedan-
strasse

Bordeaux
Platz

Belfortstr

Sülchenstr

STRASSE

ROSENHEIMER

HAIDHAUSEN

Metz-
strasse

Strasse

Ostbahnhof

OSTBAHNHOF

ROSENHEIMER
PLATZ

Weissenburger

S Brauscher

Orlean's
platz

Mühldorfstrasse

BALAN
STRASSE

Lothringerstrasse

Gravelottestr

P

FRANZISKANER-STRASSE

Berufsb
zentrum

strasse

Haager
str

strasse

Weg

Frieden-

Grafinger

STRASSE

Strasse

Sieboldstr

Jugendwohnheim

ORLEANS-

ROSENHEIMER

Salesianum

Auerfeldstrasse

BALAN
STRASSE

Bayerische
Volkssternwarte

STRASSE

P

Sankt

Cajetan-str

ANZINGER STRASSE

L

M

Deutsches Museum

HIGHLIGHTS

- Planetarium
- Karl Benz's Automobil Nummer I
- Copy of the Puffing Billy steam train
- Reconstruction of a coal mine
- Dornier Do 31 and Junkers Ju 52 aircraft
- 19th-century sailing ship— 60m (197ft) long

TIP

- The museum shop is a great source for science books, souvenirs and quality museum-endorsed gifts to appeal to all ages (tel: 21 79 224).

If you spent one minute at each exhibit, it would take you 36 days to see everything at this museum of superlatives—Munich's most famous and Germany's most visited science museum.

Voyage of discovery In 1903, engineer Oskar von Miller founded the Museum of Masterworks of Science and Technology. After his death, the collection moved to its present building on its own island on the Isar, east of the city, and was officially opened in 1925. Over the years this giant technological playground has grown to a staggering 17,000-plus exhibits, ranging from the sundial to the space shuttle.

Learning experience The most popular areas cover mining (including a reconstructed coal

The Deutsches Museum sits on its own island on the Isar and houses one of the world's greatest collections of scientific and technological exhibits

mine), computer science and various transportation sections. Alongside original objects are audiovisual displays, experiments and hands-on models.

Unique exhibits Some of the most dramatic displays are the star shows at the Planetarium (which take place in the high-tech Forum), an ear-splitting high-voltage demonstration that simulates a 220,000-volt flash of lightning, and the vast model railway on the ground level. Other highlights are a reconstruction of the caves at Lascaux; the first German U-boat (submarine); one of the first jet planes; Karl Benz's first car; a massive train track featuring many types of train; and the bench on which Otto Hahn proved the splitting of the atom. The exhibits constantly evolve to reflect the latest historical and technological discoveries.

THE BASICS

www.deutschesmuseum.de
➕ J8
🗺 Museumsinsel 1
☎ 2179-1
🕐 Daily 9–5
🍴 Restaurant, café
🚇 S-Bahn Isartor; U-Bahn Fraunhoferstrasse
🚌 131; tram 8
♿ Excellent
💪 Moderate

Asamkirche

The church of St. John Nepomuk is known as Asamkirche after its architects

THE BASICS

🔆 H7
✉ Sendlinger Strasse 32
☎ 368 7989
🕐 Mon–Fri 7.30–6, Sat 8–7, Sun 8–3
🚇 U-Bahn Sendlinger Tor
🚌 152; tram 17, 18, 27
♿ Free

HIGHLIGHTS

● Gnadenstuhl (Throne of Mercy), E. Q. Asam
● Ceiling fresco, C. D. Asam
● Two-tiered high altar
● Wax effigy of St. John Nepomuk
● Statues of John the Baptist and St. John the Evangelist
● Portraits of the Asam brothers
● Facade

The Asamkirche may be Munich's finest rococo structure. A narrow but sensational facade provides a mere hint of the sumptuous interior—one of the most lavish works of the celebrated Asam brothers.

The Asam brothers In 1729, master architect and sculptor Egid Quirin Asam acquired a house in Sendlinger Strasse and built his own private church next door, assisted by his brother, a distinguished fresco artist. For this reason, the Church of St. John Nepomuk (a Bohemian saint popular in 18th-century Bavaria) is better known as the Asamkirche. Even though Asam financed the construction, he was forced to open it to the public, and the church was consecrated in 1746. Free from the normal constraints of a patron's demands, the brothers created a dazzling jewel of rococo architecture.

Lavish decoration The unobtrusive marble facade has an unusual plinth of unhewn rocks and a kneeling figure of St. John Nepomuk. The tiny, dark but opulent interior is crammed with sculptures, murals and gold leaf, and crowned by a magnificent ceiling fresco depicting the life of the saint. The long, narrow nave carries your eye straight to the glorious two-tiered high altar and shrine of St. John Nepomuk. The gleaming gallery altar, portraying the Trinity and illuminated by an oval window representing the sun, is crowned by Egid Quirin's *Throne of Mercy*, depicting Christ crucified, in the arms of God, wearing the papal crown.

Frauenkirche

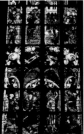

This massive, late-Gothic brick church symbolizes Munich more than any other building. Its sturdy twin towers (99m/325ft and 100m/328ft high), with their Italian-Renaissance onion domes, dominate the city's skyline.

Munich's cathedral The Frauenkirche, built between 1468 and 1488, has been the cathedral of Southern Bavaria since 1821. Today's structure, the largest reconstructed medieval building in Munich, has been rebuilt from the rubble of World War II. Little remains of the original design except the basic architectural elements and the windows in the choir. Its strength lies in its simplicity and grand proportions.

Onion domes Thirty years after the church's consecration, the towers were still roofless. In 1524, unique green Italian-Renaissance onion domes were erected as a temporary measure. With this eccentric addition to the structure, the building once provoked an irreverent comparison to a pair of beer mugs with lids. However, the domes became so popular that they were retained.

The Devil's footprint A footprint is visible in the stone floor by the entrance. Legend has it that the Devil visited the church and stamped his foot in delight because the architect had apparently forgotten to put in windows, though the building was flooded with light. But Jörg von Halsbach's ingenious design meant that no windows were visible from this point, thus giving him the last laugh.

THE BASICS

+ J7
- Frauenplatz 1
- 290 0820
- Sat–Wed 7–7, Thu 7–8.30, Fri 7–6
- U- or S-Bahn Marienplatz
- 52, 131, 152; tram 19
- None
- Free

HIGHLIGHTS

- Gothic stained-glass windows
- The Baptism of Christ, Friedrich Pacher altarpiece
- Jan Polack altar panels
- St. Lantpert's Chapel with wood figures of apostles and prophets from the workshop of Erasmus Grasser

Marienplatz and Neues Rathaus

HIGHLIGHTS

- Glockenspiel
- Facade
- Tower
- Ratskeller (▷ 42)

TIP

- Don't miss Konrad Knoll's famous Fish Fountain here, on the site of a former fish market. They say if you wash your purse here on Ash Wednesday, it will never be empty. The Lord Mayor still-washes the City Purse here every year.

Eleven o'clock is the magic hour for tourists who crowd Marienplatz to see the world-famous Munich Glockenspiel in action on the lavish neo-Gothic facade of the New Town Hall.

Towers and turrets Marienplatz is the city's main square, and traditionally the scene of tournaments, festivals and ceremonies. It is also a great place to people-watch. The entire north side of the square is dominated by the imposing Neues Rathaus (New Town Hall), seat of the city government for nearly a century. Constructed between 1867 and 1909 around six courtyards with towers and turrets, sculptures and gargoyles, its neo-Gothic style was controversial at the time, but the Neues Rathaus has since become one of Munich's best-known landmarks.

Marienplatz, with the famous Glockenspiel on the Neues Rathaus (New Town Hall), is the heart of the city

The Glockenspiel On the main front of the building, figures of Bavarian royalty stand alongside saints and characters from local folklore. The central tower viewing platform offers a fantastic view of the city, and houses one of the largest Glockenspiels (carillons) in Europe. This mechanical clock plays four different tunes on 43 bells while 32 almost life-size carved figures present scenes from Munich's history—among them the jousting match at the marriage of Duke Wilhelm V with Renate of Lorraine in 1568, and the *Schäfflertanz* (Coopers' dance) of 1517, celebrating the end of the Black Death. This dance is re-enacted in Munich's streets every seven years (next in 2018). Both Glockenspiel events can be seen daily at 11am and also at noon and at 5pm in summer. The cuckoo that ends the performance always raises a smile.

THE BASICS

- ✚ J7
- ✉ Marienplatz
- ☎ 23 300 (Neues Rathaus)
- 🕐 Tower: Nov–Apr Mon–Fri 10–5, May–Oct 10–7
- 🍴 Ratskeller beer hall and restaurant
- Ⓡ U- or S-Bahn Marienplatz
- 🚌 52, 131, 152
- ♿ Few
- 👆 Tower: inexpensive

Münchner Stadtmuseum

The City Museum is housed in the former armory

THE BASICS

www.stadtmuseum-online.de
✚ H7
✉ St.-Jakobs-Platz 1
☎ 233 22370
🕐 Tue–Sun 10–6
🍴 Café and beer garden
🚇 U-Bahn Sendlinger Tor,
U- or S-Bahn Marienplatz
🚌 52, 131, 152
♿ Good
💰 Moderate
❓ Tours, lectures

HIGHLIGHTS

● History of the City section
● Marionette Theater
Collection and fairground
museum
● Photography and Film
Museum

Munich's unique, lively, eclectic personality is reflected in the diverse nature of the City Museum's collections, which range from weapons, armor and fashion to fairgrounds, Biedermeier and films.

City history If your itinerary does not allow enough time to explore all the old parts of the city on foot, head straight to the History of the City section housed on the first floor, to study Munich's development since the Middle Ages through maps, models and before-and-after photographs, which illustrate the devastating effects of World War II bombing.

Unusual collections As the museum is housed in the former city armory, it is only fitting that it should contain one of the largest collections of ancient weaponry in Germany. Other collections worth visiting include fashion from the 18th century to the present day, the second-largest musical instrument collection in Europe and the Photography and Film Museum, with its fascinating display of ancient cameras and photographs. Don't miss the greatest treasure—Erasmus Grasser's 10 Moriske Dancers (1480), magnificent examples of late Gothic secular art, originally carved for the Old Town Hall.

For children of all ages On the third floor the Marionette Theater Collection (Münchner Marionettentheater), one of the world's largest, reflects Bavaria's role in the production of glove-puppets, shadow plays and mechanical toys.

*The tower of
Peterskirche*

Peterskirche

**Known affectionately as Alter Peter, the
city's oldest parish church is immortalized
in a traditional song that claims "Until
Old Peter's tower falls down, we'll have a
good life in Munich town."**

Built over time The Peterskirche dates from
the foundations of the city itself in 1158, on
a slight hill called the Petersbergl, where the
monks (who gave their name to Munich)
had established a settlement in the 11th century. The original Romanesque structure was
expanded in Gothic style and renovated.

Destruction and rebirth During World War II
the church was almost entirely destroyed. In an
attempt to raise money to rebuild it, Bavarian
Radio stirred the hearts of the people of Munich
by playing only a shortened version of the
"Alter Peter" song, and public donations flowed
in. After the tower was completed, in October
1951, the full version was at last heard again.

Bells and a view The most extraordinary
feature is the tower with its lantern-dome
and eight asymmetrically placed clock-faces,
designed so that, according to Karl Valentin
(▷ 35), eight people can tell the time at once.
The chimes are renowned and include one of
the largest bells in Germany: The best time to
hear them is at 3pm on Saturday, when they
ring in the Sabbath. The 306-step climb to the
viewing platform is rewarded by a dramatic
bird's-eye view of Munich.

THE BASICS

✚ J7
✉ Petersplatz
☎ 260 4828
🕐 Tower Mon–Fri 8–6.30,
Sat–Sun & Holidays
10–6.30 (closes 1hr earlier
in winter). Closed in bad
weather
🚇 U- or S-Bahn
Marienplatz
🚌 52, 131, 152
♿ None
🎫 Tower: inexpensive

HIGHLIGHTS

● High Altar (Nikolaus
Stuber, Egid Quirin Asam and
Erasmus Grasser)
● Clock tower
● Schrenk Altar
● Jan Polack's five Gothic
pictures
● Mariahilf Altar (Ignaz
Günther)
● Corpus-Christi Altar (Ignaz
Günther)
● Aresinger-Epitaph
(Erasmus Grasser)

INNENSTADT SÜD TOP 25

Jüdisches Museum

Door of the Ten
Commandments;
Synagoge und
Judisches Museum

THE BASICS

www.juedischesmuseum-
muenchen.de

🚩 H7

✉ St.-Jakobs-Platz
16, 80331

☎ 2339 6096

🕐 Tue–Sun 10–6,

🍴 Café Makom
www.cafe-makom.de
St-Jakobs-Platz 16,
24 29 37 76

🚇 U- or S-Bahn
Marienplatz

🚌 62

♿ Very good

💶 Inexpensive

❓ Library: free. Ask for
a "reader's badge" at the
information counter. A
Jewish Museum ticket stub
allows 50% off admission
to other Munich museums
for the next 48 hours.

HIGHLIGHTS

● Large interactive map of
Munich with pictures and
tales of Jewish families
● 19th-century embroidered
satin Torah cover
● Glass and steel mesh fili-
gree decoration on the New
Synagogue
● Jordan B.Gorfinkel's (Gorf)
cartoon *Everything's Relative*

**At the heart of this built-for-purpose
cultural center serving the city's growing
Jewish community is a small but engaging museum showcasing local Jewish history, religion and contemporary life.**

The Permanent Exhibition This traces Jewish
history in Munich from the early 13th century.
Eye-catching displays explaining the significance
of religious festivals such as Rosh Hashanah
(New Year), Yom Kippur (Day of Atonement),
Hanukkah (Festival of Lights) and Pesach
(Passover), as well as rituals of life (circumcision,
Bar Mitzvah, marriage and death).

Temporary Exhibitions Thought-provoking
temporary exhibitions of photography, art and
installations by contemporary Jewish artists are
enhanced by online study areas where visitors can discover more about the displays. The
museum is a center for research and holds regular discussions and presentations on aspects of
Jewish life. The extensive library, which is open to
all, has a section for genealogical research.

Community Center The terrace of the Café
Makom, serving coffee and vegetarian snacks,
is the best place to take in the architectural con-
cept; a metaphor for the Temple of Solomon.
The buildings, comprising the New Synagogue,
Community Center and Museum were designed
by Rena Wandel-Hoefer and Wolfgang Lorch. Do
not miss the comic strip silk screen panels on
the museum entrance by Chicago artist Gorf.

TOP 25

Viktualienmarkt

Less than a stone's throw from the cosmopolitan shops of Munich's main pedestrian zone, this bustling open-air food market, with taverns and cooked food stands, has retained its traditional atmosphere for centuries.

A long tradition In 1807 it was decided that the market in Marienplatz had become too small for the rapidly growing trade. So a new Viktualienmarkt was planned for a grassy field outside the city, where livestock grazed and stagecoaches stopped. Today it is Munich's oldest, largest and most attractive market with its quaint green wooden stalls and jazzy striped umbrellas.

Atmosphere The lively atmosphere of the market owes much to the robust market women, famous for the loud and lively abuse they dish out in earthy Bavarian dialect to their customers. Their goods are superb, the prices high and the variety of fresh produce is vast, ranging from Bavarian blue cheese to Alpine herbs and flowers. Look out for neatly tied bundles of asparagus in spring, and mountains of fresh cranberries in summer.

Open-air restaurant Try some Bavarian specialties from the little taverns and stands dotted around the market—*Leberkäs* (meat loaf) or a *Brat-* or *Weisswurst* (fried or white sausage)—wash it down with a typically Bavarian *Weissbier* (a light beer made using top-fermentation yeast) in the beer garden set up round the maypole, the scene of lively May Day celebrations.

THE BASICS

www.viktualienmarkt-muenchen.de

✚ J7

🕐 Mon–Fri 7.30–6, Sat 7.30–1

🍴 Numerous stands serve hot and cold snacks

🚇 U- or S-Bahn Marienplatz

🚌 52, 131, 152

HIGHLIGHTS

● Irene Schwarz—more than 40 different kinds of potato
● Exoten Müller—freshly pressed fruit juices
● Rottler–herbs, mustards, preserves and chutneys
● Münchner Suppenküche—soup kitchen (▷ 41)
● Nordsee—fish snacks (▷ 42)
● Pferdemetzgerei Wörle—specialty horsemeat sausages
● Ludwig Freisinger—herbs and spices
● Honighäusl—herbal honey wines

33

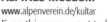

More to See

ALPINES MUSEUM

www.alpenverein.de/kultar

Everything you want to know about mountaineering in the Alps from 1760 onwards, plus occasional temporary exhibitions.

➕ K7 ✉ Praterinsel 5 ☎ 211 2240
🕐 Tue–Fri 1–6, Sat, Sun 11–6 🚇 U- or S-Bahn Isartor 🚋 Tram 17 💵 Moderate

BAYERISCHE VOLKSSTERNWARTE

www.sternwarte-muenchen.de

The Bavarian Observatory is fascinating, and a special late-night treat for children. Friendly staff will help you find specific stars and comets, and there's a show in English on Monday evenings.

➕ L9 ✉ Rosenheimer Strasse 145
☎ 40 62 39 🕐 Sep–Mar Mon–Fri 8pm–10pm; Apr–Aug Mon–Fri 9pm–11pm
🚇 U-Bahn Karl-Preis-Platz 💵 Moderate

BIER- UND OKTOBERFEST-MUSEUM

www.bier-und-oktoberfestmuseum.de

With its six breweries Munich is the world's number one beer metropolis. This special museum is devoted to beer and its famous celebration, the Oktoberfest. Learn about the history of beer and discover why Munich's is so special.

➕ J7 ✉ Sterneckerstrasse 2 ☎ 2423 1607 🕐 Tue–Sat 1–6 🚇 S-Bahn Isartor 💵 Moderate

DEUTSCHES JAGD- UND FISCHEREIMUSEUM

www.jagd-fischerei-museum.de

The German Hunting and Fishing Museum has the most important collection of its kind in Germany, including the Wolpertinger, a hoax animal resembling a marmot with webbed feet, antlers and wings.

➕ H7 ✉ Neuhauserstrasse 2 ☎ 22 05 22
🕐 Daily 9.30–5 (Thu until 9) 🚇 U- or S-Bahn Marienplatz 💵 Moderate

MARIENSÄULE

Marienplatz owes its name to this gracious figure of the Virgin Mary. All distances in Bavaria are measured from this point.

A boar guards the entrance to the Hunting and Fishing Museum

The Mariensäule and the Neues Rathaus

➕ J7 ✉ Marienplatz 🚇 U- or S-Bahn Marienplatz

MICHAELSKIRCHE
www.st-michael-muenchen.de
The largest Renaissance church north of the Alps, the Jesuit Church of St. Michael was built at the end of the 16th century by Duke Wilhelm (the Pious) as a monument to the Counter-Reformation. Disaster struck in 1590 when the tower collapsed; it was finally consecrated in 1597. War damage has been masterfully repaired. Marvel at the Renaissance hall with its ornate, barrel-vaulted roof.
➕ H7 ✉ Neuhauserstrasse 6
☎ 231 7060 🕐 Mon–Sat 10–7 (Thu until 8.45), Sun 6.50am–10.15pm 🚇 U- or S-Bahn Karlsplatz 🚋 Tram 16, 17, 18, 19, 20, 21, 27 ✋ Free

MÜLLER'SCHES VOLKSBAD
Germany's loveliest indoor swimming pool, in the Jugendstil style.
➕ K8 ✉ Rosenheimer Strasse 1 ☎ 2361 5050 🚇 S-Bahn Isartor 🚋 Tram 18

SENDLINGER TOR
The medieval Sendlinger Tor town gate space has a large central arch and two hexagonal flanking towers. It was once the southern exit of the town walls.
➕ H7 🚇 U-Bahn Sendlinger Tor

VALENTIN MUSÄUM
www.valentin-musaeum.de
A fine showcase for the eccentric and distinctive humour of Munich's Karl Valentin (1882–1948), Bavaria's answer to Charlie Chaplin, much-loved for his quirky wit and misanthropic humor. He started out by entertaining the crowds in beer halls but soon attracted the attention of Schwabing intellectuals and is perhaps best remembered for his sketch in which he put fish in a bird-cage and birds in an aquarium. The museum contains various oddities, and has bizarre opening times too.
➕ I7 ✉ Tal 50 ☎ 223266 🕐 Mon, Tue, 11.01–5.29; Fri, Sat 11.01–5.59; Sun 10.01–5.29 🚇 S-Bahn Isartor ✋ Free

Müller'sches Volksbad–a Jugendstil public bath

Munich's Old Town

Explore the pedestrian heart of Munich, between its medieval west and east gates, with its cathedral, main square and market.

DISTANCE: 2km (1.2 miles) **ALLOW:** 2 hours (excluding visits)

START

KARLSPLATZ
⊞ H7 🚇 S- and U-Bahn Karlsplatz

END

KARLSPLATZ
⊞ H7 🚇 S- and U-Bahn Karlsplatz

1 Pass through Karlstor, site of the former medieval west gate to the city, into Neuhauserstrasse, the main pedestrian shopping zone. Don't miss the Michaelskirche (▷ 35) on the left.

8 Head back along Tal towards Marienplatz. Just before entering the square, look for the Old Town Hall, which also houses a toy museum. Cross Marienplatz, continue up Neuhauserstrasse back to the startpoint.

2 Turn left on Augustenstrasse to Frauenkirche (▷ 27), the cathedral, with its distinctive onion-shape domes. Return to the main shopping area via Liebfrauenstrasse and on to Marienplatz (▷ 28–29).

7 Turn right into Westenrieder Strasse then first left up Sterneckerstrasse past the Bier-und-Oktoberfestmuseum (▷ 34). Continue on to Tal. Turn right toward Isartor, Munich's most easterly remaining medieval gate. Inside one tower is the museum devoted to Karl Valentin (▷ 35).

3 Head up Rindermarkt (beside Hugendubel bookshop ▷ 38) to the Peterskirche (▷ 31). If you're feeling energetic, climb the tower—the view of the city is worth the effort.

6 You will come to Gärtnerplatz, site of the celebrated Staatstheater (▷ 40). Proceed past the bars and restaurants of Klenzestrasse, cross Rumfordstrasse and Frauen Strasse until you reach Zwinger Strasse.

4 Swing round the side of the church to the Viktualienmarkt (▷ 33), for some light refreshment in the beer garden or from one of the small food stands there.

5 Cross to the far side of the market and continue down Reichenbachstrasse.

INNENSTADT SÜD WALK

37

Shopping

DECO SUSANNE KLEIN

A tiny boutique near Gärtnerplatz, specializing in modern furniture, plush fabrics and state-of-the-art interior design.

➕ J8 ✉ Klenzestrasse 41 ☎ 272 2427 🚇 U-Bahn Fraunhoferstrasse 🚌 52, 152

DEHNER

www.dehner.de
Full of great gift ideas for garden lovers. What about a packet of Alpine flower seeds or even a grow-your-own Bavarian meadow?

➕ J7 ✉ Frauen Strasse 8 ☎ 2423 9980 🚇 S-Bahn Isartor

DEUTSCHES MUSE-UM SHOP

www.deutsches-museum-shop.de
An amazing, eccentric shop full of books, toys, puzzles and models based on the scientific and technical world, for scientifically minded children and adults.

➕ J8 ✉ Museumsinsel 1 ☎ 2138 3892 🚇 S-Bahn Isartor 🚋 Tram 18

FOURTH DIMENSION

www.fourthdimension.de
One of Germany's leading costume jewelry shops. Smart but affordable.

➕ J7 ✉ Frauenplatz 14 ☎ 2280 1090 🚇 S-Bahn Marienplatz

GALERIA KAUFHOF

www.galeria-kaufhof.de
One of several Kaufhof department stores here; centrally located.

➕ J7 ✉ Kaufingerstrasse 1–5 ☎ 23 18 51 🚇 U- or S-Bahn Marienplatz

GESCHENKE KAISER

www.geschenke-kaiser.de
A fine range of pewter Christmas decorations, serving dishes, candle-sticks and beer jugs are the specialties here.

➕ J7 ✉ Rindermarkt 1 ☎ 26 45 09 🚇 U- or S-Bahn Marienplatz

HIRMER

www.hirmer-grosse-groessen.de
A first-class clothing shop with six floors exclusively for men.

➕ H7 ✉ Kaufingerstrasse 28 ☎ 23 68 30 🚇 U- or S-Bahn Marienplatz

HOLZ LEUTE

www.holz-leute.de
Everything here is made of wood, with decorative and functional items

BARGAIN-HUNTING

Munich has over 8,000 shops and 15 big department stores and there are plenty of bargains to be had if you know where to look. Start with the department stores that sell cut-price goods in their basements, and always keep your eyes open for *Sonderangebot* (special offer) signs. The best bargains can be found at the end-of-season sales in January and July.

ranging from games to biscuit cutters.

➕ J7 ✉ Viktualienmarkt 2 ☎ 26 82 48 🚇 U- or S-Bahn Marienplatz

HUGENDUBEL

www.hugendubel.de
A giant branch of the book chain, spread over four floors. There are even sofas where you can sit and read to your heart's content without buying! There are several more branches in the city.

➕ J7 ✉ Marienplatz 22 ☎ 3075 7575 🚇 U- or S-Bahn Marienplatz

KARSTADT

www.karstadt.de
This giant department store has six outlets in the city; this one, Haus Oberpollinger am Dom, sells electrical appliances, books, furnishings, cosmetics and clothing.

➕ H7 ✉ Neuhauserstrasse 18 ☎ 29 02 30 🚇 U- or S-Bahn Karlsplatz

KAUT-BULLINGER

www.kaut-bullinger.de
Three floors of chic stationery ranging from pens, writing paper and art materials to leather personal organizers and designer wrapping paper.

➕ J7 ✉ Rosenstrasse 8 ☎ 23 80 00 🚇 U- or S-Bahn Marienplatz

KONEN

www.konen.de
A reliable fashion shop full of leading interna-

tional labels for women, men and children.

➕ H7 ✉ Sendlinger Strasse 3 ☎ 244 4220 🚇 U-Bahn Sendlinger Tor

LEDERHOSEN WAGNER

This traditional shop has been making Bavaria's distinctive leather shorts from soft deerskin since 1825. Surprise your friends with a shaving brush hat, made out of chamois hair, to match the shorts.

➕ J7 ✉ Tal 2 ☎ 22 56 97 🚇 U- or S-Bahn Marienplatz

LUDWIG BECK

www.ludwigbeck.com
Beck is without doubt Munich's most stylish department store. At Christmas artisans work on the top floor and the store becomes a winter wonderland of handicrafts.

➕ J7 ✉ Theatinerstrasse 14 ☎ 23 69 10 🚇 U- or S-Bahn Marienplatz

MAX KRUG

www.max krug.com
Old Bavaria lives on in this trove of traditional souvenirs and knick-knacks—handmade wooden cuckoo clocks, beer steins and more.

➕ H7 ✉ Neuhauserstrasse 2 ☎ 22 45 01 🚇 U- or S-Bahn Karlsplatz

MESSER & SCHEREN

A specialist knife and scissor shop—excellent for left-handers too.

➕ K8 ✉ Rosenheimer Strasse 42 ☎ 480 1392 🚇 S-Bahn Rosenheimer Platz

OBLETTER

www.obletter.de
Comprehensive toy shop selling everything from cuddly toys to train sets. Other branches.

➕ H7 ✉ Karlsplatz 11–12 ☎ 5508 9510 🚇 U- or S-Bahn Karlsplatz

RISCHART

www.rischart.de
One of many Rischart shops offers the largest choice of bread, rolls and cakes in town.

➕ J7 ✉ Marienplatz 18 ☎ 231 7000 🚇 U- or S-Bahn Marienplatz

SCHMIDT

Shop here for some of the best *Lebkuchen*

(delicious gingerbread), which are presented in collectable tins, along with *Stollen* (traditional festive fruitcakes).

➕ J7 ✉ Westenrieder-strasse 6 ☎ 2323 8980 🚇 S-Bahn Isartor

SPANISCHES FRUCHTHAUS

A mouth-watering display of dried fruits entices you into this small shop with an unusual selection of crystallized, fresh and chocolate-coated fruits.

➕ J7 ✉ Rindermarkt 10 ☎ 26 45 70 🚇 U- or S-Bahn Marienplatz

SPORTSCHECK

The department store for sports fanatics. Six floors are dedicated to every sport imaginable. It's just an hour by car to the nearest ski slopes, and the store will even arrange day-long ski trips to the mountains.

➕ H7 ✉ Neuhauser Strasse 21 ☎ 21660 🚇 U- or S-Bahn Karlsplatz

VIKTUALIENMARKT

www.viktualienmarkt-muenchen.de
The largest and most famous Bavarian open-air food market, look out for the Kräuter-Freisinger stand for herbs and the Honighäusl stand for honey products. There are plenty of opportunites to try beer and food too.

➕ J7 🕐 Mon–Fri 7.30–6, Sat 7.30–1 🚇 U- or S-Bahn Marienplatz

Entertainment and Nightlife

CAFÉ GLOCKENSPIEL

www.cafe-glockenspiel.de
Opposite Marienplatz's famous Glockenspiel (▷ 28–29), the roof-terrace cocktail bar and 1970s-style Espresso bar-café here are always crowded.
➕ J7 ✉ Marienplatz 28 (5th floor) ☎ 26 42 56 🕙 10am–1am 🚇 U- or S-Bahn Marienplatz

GASTEIG

www.gasteig.de
Home of the Munich Philharmonic Orchestra and the city's main cultural hub, offering a rich program of events.
➕ K8 ✉ Rosenheimerstrasse 5 ☎ 48 09 80 🚇 S-Bahn Rosenheimer Platz

HAVANA CLUB

www.havanaclub-muenchen.de
There are over 100 types of rum on sale at this intimate bar. It's decorated in rich Spanish colonial style, with pictures of Ernest Hemingway on the walls.
➕ J7 ✉ Herrnstrasse 30 ☎ 29 18 84 🕙 Mon–Thu 6pm–1am, Fri–Sat 6pm–3am, Sun 7pm–1am 🚇 S-Bahn Isartor

HOLY HOME

Popular locals bar near trendy Gärtnerplatz, where the music is as eclectic as the décor; a great night out.
➕ J8 ✉ Reichenbachstrasse 21 ☎ 201 4546 🕙 7pm–2am (Fri–Sat til 3am) 🚇 U-Bahn Fraunhoferstrasse 🚌 152

ICE RINK

Skate under the stars on this outdoor ice rink. Skate rental is available, and the rink is surrounded by stands selling snacks such as steaming *glühwein*.
➕ H7 ✉ Karlsplatz 🕙 Late Nov–Jan daily 10.30–10 🚇 U- or S-Bahn Marienplatz

MASTER'S HOME

www.mastershome-muenchen.de
An extraordinary underground bar in the colonial style of a typical African farmhouse. Sit in the bathroom, the bedroom, the living room or at the bar, which is cooled by a giant aeroplane propeller, and eat, dance or simply lap up the atmosphere over a delicious cocktail.
➕ J7 ✉ Frauenstrasse 11 ☎ 22 99 09 🕙 Daily 6pm–2am 🚇 S-Bahn Isartor

MÜNCHNER FILMMUSEUM

www.stadtmuseum-online.de/filmmu.htm
Join an eclectic crowd

ALL-NIGHT PARTYING

Compared with some cities, Munich's nightlife is small-scale and provincial. Due to early-closing laws, most bars close around 1am and most nightclubs at 4am. However, the Backstage Club, nicknamed House of the Rising Sun, with its techno and house music sometimes doesn't even open until 6am.

for screenings (Tuesday–Sunday) from Germany's largest collection of silent movies.
➕ H7 ✉ St.-Jakobs-Platz 1 ☎ 2332 2370 🚇 U-Bahn Sendlinger Tor, U- or S-Bahn Marienplatz

MUSEUM LICHTSPIELE

www.movietown.eu
This former music hall frequently shows English-language films.
➕ K8 ✉ Lilienstrasse 2 ☎ 482403 🚇 S-Bahn Rosenheimer Platz 🚃 Tram 27

ODODO

A simple, stylish bar with a convivial atmosphere, appealing to a diverse clientele, for its unusual mix of fondues and exotic cocktails.
➕ J8 ✉ Buttermelcherstrasse 6 ☎ 260 7741 🕙 Mon–Thu 11am–1am, Fri 11am–3am, Sat 6pm–3am, Sun 6pm–1am 🚇 U-Bahn Fraunhoferstrasse 🚃 Tram 17, 18

STAATSTHEATER AM GÄRTNERPLATZ

www.staatstheater-am-gaertnerplatz.de
This flourishing theater claims to be the only municipal light opera house in the world, with a wide repertoire of operetta, light opera, musicals and ballet.
➕ J8 ✉ Gärtnerplatz 3 ☎ 202411 🚇 U-Bahn Fraunhoferstrasse 🚃 52, 56

Restaurants

PRICES

Prices are approximate, based on a 3-course meal for one person.

€€€	over €50
€€	€25–€50
€	under €25

ADAMELLO (€)

Hidden in a quiet backstreet in Haidhausen, this Italian-run café sells the best ice cream in town. The specialty—*Coppa Adamello*—containing a mountain liqueur, is delicious.

🔶 L8 ✉ Preysingstrasse 29 ☎ 48 32 83 ◐ Daily 11–6 (midnight in summer) 🚃 Tram 18

AUGUSTINER GASTSTÄTTEN (€€)

www.augustiner-restaurant.com
Munich's oldest still-standing brewery, now a popular inn, serves reasonably priced Bavarian fare. Beer was brewed here until 1897.

🔶 H7 ✉ Neuhauserstrasse 27 ☎ 2318 3257 🚇 U- or S-Bahn Karlsplatz

CAFÉ FRISCHHUT (€)

Early birds meet night owls for strong coffee and delicious deep-fried *Schmalznudeln* donuts as early as 5 in the morning. Great for relaxing and people-watching.

🔶 J7 ✉ Prälat-Zistl-Strasse 8 ☎ 2602 3156 ◐ Mon–Fri 7–6, Sat 5–5 🚇 U- or S-Bahn Marienplatz

CAFÉ GLOCKENSPIEL (€€€)

www.cafe-glockenspiel.de
One of Munich's most romantic settings directly opposite the Glockenspiel. There's also a popular café and bar (▷ 40).

🔶 J7 ✉ Marienplatz 28 ☎ 26 42 56 ◐ Restaurant daily 10–11.30. Café daily 10–1 🚇 U- or S-Bahn Marienplatz

CAFÉ HAIDHAUSEN (€)

Look out for the Hangover breakfast or try the romantic Romeo and Juliet breakfast for two, served until 4pm.

🔶 K8 ✉ Franziskanerstrasse 4 ☎ 688 6043 🚇 S-Bahn Rosenheimer Platz

JOE PEÑA'S (€€)

www.joepenas.com
This Mexican restaurant is always packed due to its

RUSTIC ATMOSPHERE

Wooden tables covered with blue-and-white check tablecloths, benches and carved chairs lend a warm feel to a typical Bavarian restaurant. Murals depicting mountains, lakes and hunting scenes are hung on the walls next to prized antlers or a collection of beer mugs. Try some *Weisswürste* (white sausages) or hearty *Schweinebraten* (roast pork) with sauerkraut and *Knödel* (dumplings) while you soak up the atmosphere.

delicious fajitas, burritos and tequilas.

🔶 J8 ✉ Buttermelcherstrasse 17 ☎ 22 64 63 ◐ Dinner only 5pm–1am

KÖNIGSHOF (€€€)

www.koenigshof-hotel.de
In one of Munich's finest hotels, sample tempting regional delicacies and an extensive wine list in an elegant setting overlooking Karlsplatz.

🔶 H7 ✉ Karlsplatz 25 ☎ 55 13 60 ◐ Closed Sun 🚇 U- or S-Bahn Karlsplatz

MAREDO (€€)

www.maredo.de
The best steak and salad in town is only a stone's throw from Marienplatz.

🔶 J7 ✉ Rindermarkt 5 ☎ 2607410 ◐ Daily 11.30–11.30 (Fri–Sat til 12) 🚇 U- or S-Bahn Marienplatz

MASTER'S HOME (€€€)

www.mastershome-muenchen.de
Sit in the bar and enjoy a pizza from the wood-fired oven in the master's kitchen. Or try the 8-course tasting menu in the luxurious dining room. Either will be a memorable experience.

🔶 J7 ✉ Frauenstrasse 11 ☎ 22 99 09 ◐ Daily 6–late 🚇 S-Bahn Isartor

MÜNCHNER SUPPENKÜCHE (€)

www.muenchner-suppenkueche.com
Try the *Pfannkuchensuppe* (pancake soup) or

Leberknödelsuppe (liver dumpling soup) at this soup kitchen.
⊞ J7 ⊠ Viktualienmarkt ☎ 5527 3390 ⊙ Shop hours ⊜ U- or S-Bahn Marienplatz

NORDSEE (€)
www.nordsee.de
This fast-food fish eatery offers a range of hot and cold dishes. There's standing room only.
⊞ J7 ⊠ Viktualienmarkt ☎ 22 11 86 ⊙ Mon–Fri 8–7, Sat 8–4 ⊜ U- or S-Bahn Marienplatz

NÜRNBERGER BRATWURST GLÖCKL (€)
www.bratwurst-gloeckl.de
An ancient tavern, best known for its *Nürnberger Bratwurst* grilled over an open beechwood fire and served with sauerkraut.
⊞ J7 ⊠ Frauenplatz 9 ☎ 2919 450 ⊙ Daily 10am–midnight ⊜ U- or S-Bahn Marienplatz

PRINZ MYSHKIN (€€)
www.prinzmyshkin.com
Trendy café with a menu of creative vegetarian dishes. Don't miss the tofu stroganoff or the *involtini*, chard roulades filled with nuts and tofu.
⊞ J7 ⊠ Hackenstrasse 2 ☎ 26 55 96 ⊙ Daily 9.30–1am ⊜ U- or S-Bahn Marienplatz

RATSKELLER (€€)
www.ratskeller.com
Good solid cuisine under the vaulted arches of the New Town Hall's cellar.

⊞ J7 ⊠ Marienplatz 8 ☎ 2199 890 ⊙ Daily 9.30–1am ⊜ U- or S-Bahn Marienplatz

RUE DES HALLES (€€€)
www.rue-des-halles.de
Sophisticated, Parisian dining in Haidhausen.
⊞ L8 ⊠ Steinstrasse 18 ☎ 48 56 75 ⊙ Dinner only ⊜ S-Bahn Rosenheimer Platz

SCHLEMMERMEYER (€)
Hearty Bavarian specialties, including *Weisswurst* and *Leberkäs*, served in big portions, with mugs of Glühwein in winter.
⊞ J7 ⊠ Viktualienmarkt ☎ 295575 ⊙ Shop hours ⊜ U- or S-Bahn Marienplatz

SPEZLWIRTSCHAFT (€€)
www.spezlwirtschaft.de
Schnitzels, Käsespätzle and other traditional fare

MAHLZEIT!
Mahlzeiten (mealtimes) are comparatively early in Munich, because most people start work early (around 7–8am). Lunch is eaten between 11.30 and 2 and is for many the main meal of the day, followed by a light supper or *Abendbrot* ("evening bread"). Restaurants usually serve dinner between 6.30 and 11pm when it is polite to wish fellow diners *"Guten Appetit."* However, during the day it is more common to hear the word *"Mahlzeit."*

---

in a large, lively dining area. At weekends head for the dance club below.
⊞ J7 ⊠ Ledererstrasse 3 ☎ 23232973 ⊙ Tue–Sat 6.30pm–3am ⊜ U- or S-Bahn Marienplatz

VINAIOLO (€€)
www.vinaiolo.de
A top-notch Italian restaurant, located in fashionable Haidhausen.
⊞ L8 ⊠ Steinstrasse 42 ☎ 4895 0356 ⊙ Sun–Fri noon–3, 6.30–1, Sat 6.30–1 ⊜ S-Bahn Rosenheimer Platz ⊟ Tram 15, 25

VINCENZ MURR (€)
Help yourself at the extensive salad bar, then have a picnic by the fountain opposite.
⊞ J7 ⊠ Rosenstrasse 7 ☎ 260 4765 ⊙ Mon–Sat 8–8 ⊜ U- or S-Bahn Marienplatz

WEISSES BRÄUHAUS (€)
www.weisses-brauhaus.de
The *Weisswürste* here are easily the best in town, accompanied by a wickedly strong *Weissbier*.
⊞ J7 ⊠ Tal 7 ☎ 2901 380 ⊙ Daily 8am–1am ⊜ U- or S-Bahn Marienplatz

ZUM ALTEN MARKT (€€–€€€)
www.zumaltenmarkt.de
An Alpine-style restaurant, where traditional Bavarian meat and fish is served in daunting quantities.
⊞ J7 ⊠ Dreifaltigkeitsplatz 3 (at Viktualienmarkt) ☎ 29 99 95 ⊙ Mon–Sat 11am–midnight

Innenstadt Nord

Soak up the city's unique charm and atmosphere from the royal Residenz to the cobbled streets of the Altstadt surrounding the Hofbräuhaus, and browse in the city's most exclusive shops.

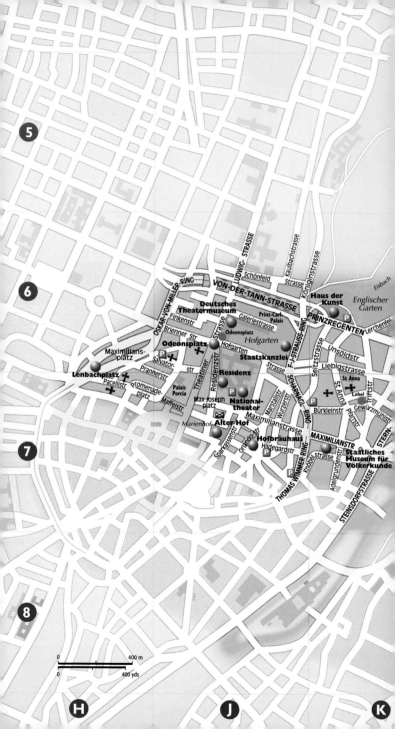

5

6

7

8

LUDWIG-STRASSE

Schönfeld Strasse

Kaulbachstrasse

Königinstrasse

Eisbach

OSKAR-VON-MILLER-RING

VON-DER-TANN-STRASSE

Haus der Kunst

Englischer Garten

Lerchenfel

PRINZREGENTEN

Deutsches Theatermuseum

Finkenstr

Brienner Str

Galeriestrasse

Prinz-Carl-Palais

Strasse

Odeonsplatz

Hofgarten

Odeonsplatz

Unsöldstr

F-J-STRAUSS-RING

Maximilians-platz

Salvator.

Theatiner

str

Hofgarten

Staatskanzlei

Seitzstrasse

Liebigstrasse

Lenbachplatz

Pranherstr

Pacellistr

Promenade-platz

Palais Porcia

Residenzstr

Strasse

Residenz

St Anna

St Anna

Lehel

Triftstr

Maffeistr

Max-Joseph-platz

National-theater

SCHARNAGL-RING

Marstallstr

Wurzerstr

Bürkleinstr

Gewürzmühlstr

Pfarrstr

MAXIMILIANSTR

STERN-

Marienhof

Alter Hof

Maximilianstrasse

Sparkassenstr

Orlando str

Hofbräuhaus

Hildegardstr

THOMAS-WIMMER-RING

Knöbel strasse

Staatliches Museum für Völkerkunde

Adelgundenstr

STEINSDORFSTRASSE

0   400 m

0   400 yds

H   **J**   **K**

Innenstadt Nord

Archäologische Staatssammlung
Bayerisches Nationalmuseum
Schack-Galerie
Friedensengel
Europa-platz
Museum Villa Stuck
Strasse
STRASSE
WIDENMAYERSTRASSE
OETTINGEN STRASSE
STRASSE
Reitmorstrasse
WIDENMAYERSTRASSE
Isar
Maximilian-anlagen
Pallas Athene
MAXIMILIANS-BRÜCKE
MAX-PLANCK-STR
Bayer Landtag
Maria-Theresia-Strasse
Möhl strasse
ISMANINGER STRASSE
ISMANINGER STRASSE
Cu-villiés-strasse
Herschelstrasse
Holbein-strasse
Geibel-str
Schumannstrasse
Lamont strasse
Possart strasse
Keplerstrasse
Kopernikusstr
PRINZREGENTEN-STRASSE
Mühlbaur-strasse
Zaubzer-str
Prinzregenten-platz
Prinzrege Theater
Nigerstrasse
Schneckenburger-strasse
Grahn-Str
GRILLPARZERSTRASSE
Versailler Str
Max-Weber-Platz
EINSTEIN-STRASSE
Strassen-bahn-Dir
Markt am Wiener Platz
Kirchen-strasse
Metzger-strasse
Seeriederstr
Leonhardstr
Flur-Strasse
Lucile-
L
M

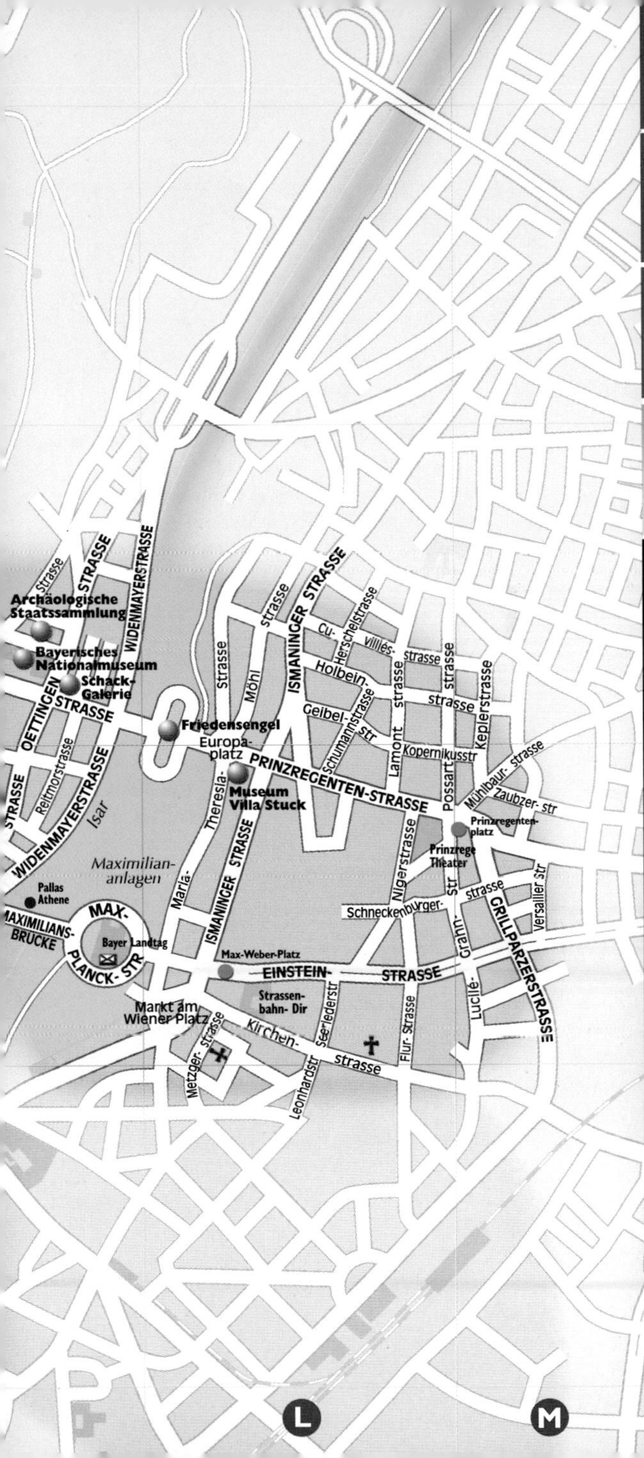

Bayerisches Nationalmuseum

The Bavarian National Museum was founded by Maximilian II in the 19th century

THE BASICS

www.bayerisches-national museum.de
➕ K6
✉ Prinzregentenstrasse 3
☎ 211 24 01
🕐 Tue–Sun 10–5 (Thu until 8pm)
🚇 U-Bahn Lehel
🚌 100; tram 17
♿ Good
💰 Moderate; Sun inexpensive

HIGHLIGHTS

● 16th-century model of Munich, by master wood-carver Jakob Sandtner
● Augsburg Weaving Room
● Tilman Riemenschneider sculptures
● Crib collection
● Flanders Tapestry Room
● Weaponry Room
● Closet from Palais Tattenbach

The Bavarian National Museum is one of Europe's leading museums of folk art, and is guaranteed to give you a real taste of Bavarian life over the centuries to the present day.

Wittelsbach treasures Thanks to the Wittelsbach rulers' passion for collecting works of art, this museum was founded in 1885 by Maximilian II and transferred to its present site in 1900. Even the building mirrors the various periods represented within the museum: the west wing is Romanesque, the east wing Renaissance, the tower baroque and the west end rococo. The interior is divided into two main collections—Folklore and Art History—providing a comprehensive survey of German cultural history, both sacred and secular, from the early Middle Ages to the present.

Folklore A series of rooms authentically decorated with rustic Bavarian furniture, glass, pottery and woodcraft provides a wonderful insight into the country life of bygone years. The Augsburg Room, with its outstanding carved ceiling, is particularly attractive. The museum is famous for its sculptures by Hans Leinberger, Ignaz Günther and Tilman Riemenschneider and its large crib collection.

Art history This collection consists of a series of specialist departments including Bavarian *Trachten* (traditional costume), tapestries, porcelain, jewelry, armor and the largest ivory collection in Europe.

No trip to Munich is complete without a visit to the Hofbräuhaus, despite its being a tourist honeypot, to sip a cool beer in the shady courtyard or in the lively beer hall. The Hofbräuhaus was founded by Wilhelm V in 1589.

Royal beer The brewery produced a special dark ale for Wilhelm's court, because he disliked the expensive local beer. Beer in Bavaria had been considered an aristocratic drink ever since the harsh winters of the 14th century destroyed the Bavarian vineyards. The ordinary citizens were unable to taste this royal brew until 1828, when the brewery finally became an inn.

Battle of the Hofbräuhaus The first mass meeting of the National Socialist Workers' Party (later the Nazi Party) was held in the Hofbräuhaus in 1920. It soon became regarded as the city's most prestigious political beer-hall arena. Here Hitler established himself as a powerful orator. On 4 November 1921, his storm troops first gained notoriety in a huge brawl, later known as the *Schlacht im Hofbräuhaus* (Battle of the Hofbräuhaus). Despite the hurling of chairs and beer mugs, Hitler finished his speech.

World's most famous pub Undoubtedly the city's best-known institution after the Oktoberfest, and a meeting place for visitors from all over the world, the Hofbräuhaus—with its long tables, buxom dirndl-clad waitresses and jolly Bavarian music—is a must for tourists.

THE BASICS

www.hofbraeuhaus.de
🚲 J7
✉ Am Platzl 9
☎ 2901 3610
🕐 Daily 9am–11.30pm.
Brass band 11am–3pm,
5.30–midnight
Ⓠ U- or S-Bahn
Marienplatz
🚌 52, 131; tram 19
♿ Good

DID YOU KNOW?

● The Hofbräuhaus is the world's most famous pub.
● The Munich Beer Regulations of 1487 are the oldest written food laws in the world.
● Bavaria is home to some 600 breweries.
● The Hofbräuhaus has its very own drinking song: *"In München steht ein Hofbräuhaus, eins, zwei, drei, g'soffa"*… (one, two, three and down the hatch).

Nationaltheater

The fully restored Nationaltheater, inside and out

THE BASICS

www.bayerische.staatsoper.de
✚ J7
✉ Max-Joseph-Platz 2
☎ 21 85 01
🕐 Box office Mon–Sat 10–7
✉ Marstallplatz 5
☎ 21 85 19 20
🚇 U- or S-Bahn Marienplatz, U-Bahn Odeonsplatz
🚌 52, 100; tram 19
♿ Few
🎧 Tour: moderate

HIGHLIGHTS

Outside
● Facade
● Pediment with Apollo and the Muses, Georg Brenninger, 1972
● Pediment with glass mosaic of *Pegasus with the Horae*, Leo Schwanthaler, 19th century
Inside
● Auditorium
● Royal box
● High-tech stage machinery and backstage equipment
● Prompter's box
● Foyer

Munich's Nationaltheater ranks among the world's leading opera houses. One of the few German theaters to have been restored to its magnificent pre-war grandeur, it is definitely worth the visit, even if opera is not your scene.

People's opera house The Nationaltheater has been home to the world-famous Bayerische Staatsoper (Bavarian State Opera) since 1818. After wartime bombing its distinguished Greek-temple design with a simple colonnaded facade stood in ruins for years until a group of citizens raised sufficient funds to restore it to its former glory. It was reopened in 1963.

Behind the scenes Most days at 2pm, during a fascinating tour, it is possible to take a rare glimpse backstage. The grandiose auditorium, with five tiers of seating decorated in plush red, gold, ivory and dove blue, is crowned by an enormous chandelier, which magically disappears into the ceiling when the curtain rises. The impressive foyer rooms provide an elegant setting for the audience to promenade in their finery.

Opening nights Many important operas have been premiered here over the centuries, including five by Wagner during the reign of Ludwig II, and many eminent artists have conducted, directed and performed here in a repertoire ranging from traditional Munich favorites—Mozart, Wagner and Strauss—to new commissions from contemporary German composers.

*Views of Feldherrnhalle
and Theatinerkirche on
Odeonsplatz*

TOP 25

Odeonsplatz

Monumental buildings surround this spacious square at the start of the city's two finest boulevards. Rubbing the noses of the lions guarding the entrance to the Residenz is said to bring good luck.

Grand plan for urban expansion Ludwig I entrusted the layout of Odeonsplatz to Leo von Klenze in the early 19th century to demonstrate the wealth of his flourishing kingdom. It also shows Klenze's passion for Renaissance Italy. His neoclassical Leuchtenberg-Palais (today the Bavarian Ministry of Finance) was inspired by Rome's Palazzo Farnese, and set the pattern for the development of the magnificent Ludwigstrasse.

Feldherrnhalle Apart from the striking Theatinerkirche—Bavaria's first baroque building and for many the most beautiful church in Munich—perhaps the most imposing building in Odeonsplatz is the Feldherrnhalle (Military Commander's Hall). It was commissioned by Ludwig I, and designed by Friedrich von Gärtner as a tribute to the Bavarian army, and adorned with statues of Bavarian generals. Note the faces of the two bronze lions: one is said to be growling at the Residenz while the other, facing the church, remains silent.

The Court Garden The peaceful Hofgarten—a park beside Odeonsplatz—retains its original 17th-century Italian layout of beautifully tended flowerbeds and fountains.

THE BASICS

➕ J6
🍴 Hofgarten Café
🚇 U-Bahn Odeonsplatz
🚌 100

HIGHLIGHTS

● Theatinerkirche
● Feldherrnhalle
● Hofgarten
● Leuchtenberg-Palais
● Odeon
● Ludwig I monument
● Preysing Palais
● Staatskanzlei (▷ 53)

INNENSTADT NORD TOP 25

Residenz

HIGHLIGHTS

- Cuvilliés-Theater
- Schatzkammer
- Antiquarium
- Ahnengalerie
- Hofkapelle
- Egyptian Art Museum
- Coin Museum

TIP

● Try to attend one of the summer open-air concerts at the Residenz, held in the atmospheric Brunnenhof courtyard. Contact München Ticket (tel: 0180 5481 8181).

The glittering staterooms of this magnificent palace demonstrate the power and wealth of the Wittelsbach dynasty—five centuries of dukes, prince-electors and kings.

Historical evolution Despite devastating damage in World War II, the Residenz was painstakingly reconstructed over four decades to its original state: a harmonious fusion of Renaissance, baroque, rococo and neoclassical styles. As you explore the 112 grand rooms crammed with priceless treasures, you can trace the centuries of architectural development, as well as the history and lifestyles of the great Wittelsbach family dynasty.

Palace highlights It would take a full day to see everything; if time is limited just see the

Munich's former ducal palace and gardens, the Residenz and Hofgarten, were begun by the Wittelsbachs in 1385 and contain the Antiquarium, the oldest German museum of Greek antiquities

Ahnengalerie (Ancestral Portrait Gallery), hung with paintings of 121 members of the Wittelsbach family; the Hofkapelle and the Reiche Kapelle, two intimate chapels (one for the courtiers and the other for the royal family); the Brunnenhof courtyard with its magnificent fountain; the unusual shell-encrusted Grottenhof courtyard; and the Antiquarium, the largest Renaissance vaulted hall in northern Europe.

Jewel in the crown The restored Cuvilliés-Theater, jewel of the Residenz and the world's finest rococo theater, is a dazzling spectacle. Built in 1750, it hosted the première of Mozart's *Idomeneo* in 1781. Also, visit the Schatzkammer (Treasury) to see the crown jewels and one of the most valuable collections of ecclesiastical and secular treasures in Europe, spanning a thousand years.

THE BASICS

www.residenz-muenchen.de
✚ J7
✉ Residenzstrasse/ Max-Joseph-Platz 3
☎ 29 06 71
🕐 Daily 10–5 (9–6 in summer)
Ⓠ U- or S-Bahn Marienplatz, U-Bahn Odeonsplatz
🚌 100; tram 19
♿ Good
⚜ Moderate

More to See

ALTER HOF

www.alter-hof-muenchen.de

With its picturesque tower, oriel window and cobbled courtyard, the Alter Hof was the royal residence (and home to the German Emperor, Ludwig IV, from 1328) from the late 12th century until the Residenz was built in the late 14th century. Today, part of the complex contains a restaurant and wine cellar.

➕ J7 ✉ Burgstrasse 8 🚇 U-Bahn Marienplatz

ARCHÄOLOGISCHE STAATSSAMMLUNG

www.archaeologie-bayern.de

The Archaeological Collection focuses on the periods from the Early Stone Age to the Middle Ages, exhibiting everyday possessions, sacred art and burial objects discovered in Bavaria.

➕ K6 ✉ Lerchenfeldstrasse 2 ☎ 211 4468 🕐 Tue–Sun 9.30–5.30 🚇 U-Bahn Lehel 🚋 Tram 17 ✋ Inexpensive

DEUTSCHES THEATERMUSEUM

www.deutschestheatermuseum.de

This small but fascinating display of set designs, costumes, photographs and props brings Germany's rich theatrical past to life.

➕ J6 ✉ Galeriestrasse 4a ☎ 2106 9128 🕐 Tue–Sun 10–4 🚇 U-Bahn Odeonsplatz ✋ Moderate

FRIEDENSENGEL

The golden Angel of Peace, high above the River Isar, was built for the 25th anniversary of Germany's victory over France in 1871.

➕ L6 ✉ Prinzregentenstrasse 🚌 100; tram 18

HAUS DER KUNST

www.hauskunst.de

This monstrous Nazi building—one of the few that Allied bombardments missed—was nicknamed the *Weisswurst* (white sausage) gallery by Hitler's opponents, because of its crude neoclassical columns. This pseudo-Classical building, designed by Paul Ludwig Troost, was the

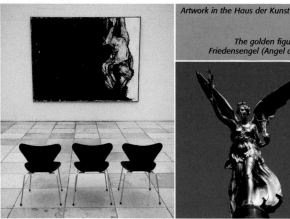

Artwork in the Haus der Kunst

The golden figure of the Friedensengel (Angel of Peace)

first monumental Nazi building in Munich, and set the pattern for later designs. Today, it provides a forum for modern art exhibitions.

➕ K6 ✉ Prinzregentenstrasse 1
☎ 2112 7113 🕐 Daily 10–8 (Thu until 10) 🚇 U-Bahn Lehel 🚌 100; tram 17
✋ Varies: moderate to expensive

LENBACHPLATZ
In this busy square is Munich's loveliest neoclassical fountain (1895). Its two figures symbolize the destructive and healing power of water.

➕ H6 ✉ Lenbachplatz 🚇 U-Bahn Karlsplatz

MUSEUM VILLA STUCK
www.villastuck.de

This stunning Jugendstil villa, the former home of artist Franz von Stuck, has been beautifully restored and contains changing exhibitions dedicated to 20th-century art.

➕ L7 ✉ Prinzregentenstrasse 60 ☎ 4555 5125 🕐 Tue–Sun 11–6 🚇 U Bahn Prinzregentenplatz 🚌 100; tram 18
✋ Inexpensive

SCHACK-GALERIE
www.pinakothek.de

This intimate gallery captures the spirit of 19th-century German art.

➕ K6 ✉ Prinzregentenstrasse 9
☎ 238 0520 🕐 Tue–Sun 10–6 (Wed til 8) 🚇 U-Bahn Lehel 🚌 100; tram 18
✋ Inexpensive

STAATSKANZLEI
The gleaming glass-and-steel Bavarian State Chancellery building is framed by a Renaissance-style arcade. The dome of the former Army Museum is its focal point.

➕ J6 ✉ Hofgarten 🚇 U-Bahn Odeonsplatz

STAATLICHES MUSEUM FÜR VÖLKERKUNDE
www.voelkerkundemuseum-muenchen.de

This museum of ethnography holds 150,000 exhibits, displayed by region—South America, Africa, India, Oceania and the Islamic Orient.

➕ K7 ✉ Maximilianstrasse 42
☎ 210 1361 00 🕐 Tue–Sun 9.30–5.30
🍴 Café 🚇 U-Bahn Lehel ✋ Moderate

The Renaissance-style arcade of the Staatskanzlei

Royal Munich

Wind the clocks back and stroll through Royal Munich with its maze of attractive cobbled streets and royal residences.

DISTANCE: 1.3km (0.8 miles) **ALLOW:** 1 hour (excluding visits)

START

ODEONSPLATZ (▷ 49)
➕ J6 🚇 U-Bahn Odeonsplatz

END

ENGLISCHER GARTEN (▷ 64–65)
➕ K4 🚇 U-Bahn Universität

1 From Odeonsplatz walk down Theatinerstrasse, with its glitzy boutiques. Turn left at Marien-hof then first right into Dienerstrasse past Alois Dallmayr—the former royal delicatessen—to Marienplatz (▷ 28–29).

8 The famous Englischer Garten (English Garden) (▷ 64–65) is just a stone's throw from the gallery. Head towards the Love Temple, one of the park's great landmarks, for splendid views of Munich's skyline.

2 From the Old Town Hall, go down Burgstrasse (beside Beck department store), the oldest street in the city, past homes of former residents Mozart and Cuvilliés.

7 Cut diagonally across the gardens, past the Staatskanzlei (▷ 53), finished in 1994, and continue down a narrow path alongside the Dichtergarten (Poets' Garden). Cross Von-der-Tann-Strasse by the pedestrian subway to the Haus der Kunst (▷ 52).

3 Go through the archway of the old royal residence (Alter Hof ▷ 52) and turn right past the Central Mint (Münzhof) along Pfisterstrasse to soak up some true Bavarian atmosphere at the Hofbräuhaus (▷ 47).

6 Head up Residenzstrasse, past the Residenz (▷ 50–51) on your right. Returning to Odeonsplatz, head eastwards into the enchanting Hofgarten (Court Garden), with its fountains and formal flowerbeds.

4 On leaving the main entrance of the Hofbräuhaus, turn right through Platzl and past Am Kosttor up to the bright lights and dazzling designer windows of exclusive Maximilianstrasse.

5 Turn left at Maximilianstrasse towards the magnificently illuminated Nationaltheater (▷ 48) at Max-Joseph-Platz.

Shopping

ANTIKE UHREN EDER
www.uhreneder.ch
The silence of this beautiful shop is broken only by the ticking of valuable German timepieces dating from the 19th and early 20th centuries. A must for collectors.
🔢 J6 ✉ Prannerstrasse 4
☎ 22 03 05 🚇 U- or S-Bahn Karlsplatz

BEHRINGER
www.behringer-schuhe.com
Fine shoes and accessories for men and women, from Prada to Jimmy Choo, in one of Germany's top shoe shops.
🔢 J6 ✉ Salvatorplatz 4
☎ 29 59 55 🚇 U-Bahn Odeonsplatz

BOETTNER
One of Munich's oldest hostelries is well known for its schnapps, caviar and other delicacies.
🔢 J7 ✉ Pfisterstrasse 9
☎ 22 12 10 🚇 U- or S-Bahn Marienplatz

BOGNER
This classic Munich company sells everything from sports clothes to traditional costumes for both men and women.
🔢 J7 ✉ Residenzstrasse 14–15 ☎ 290 7040
🚇 U- or S-Bahn Marienplatz

BREE
www.bree.com
Smart suitcases, belts, handbags and more.
🔢 J6 ✉ Theatinerhof, Salvatorstrasse 2 ☎ 29 87 45
🚇 U-Bahn Odeonsplatz

BUTLERS
www.butlers-international.de
A fun shop, full of tempting ideas for holiday gifts, including fun household gadgets and knick-knacks.
🔢 J7 ✉ Theatinerstrasse 14, Fünf Höfe ☎ 2423 1293
🚇 U-Bahn Odeonsplatz

DALLMAYR
www.dallmayr.de
Alois Dallmayr, the city's top delicatessen, famed for its mouth-watering displays, used to supply the Bavarian royal family. The first floor serves a lovely champagne breakfast.
🔢 J7 ✉ Dienerstrasse 14–15 ☎ 2135100 🚇 U- or S-Bahn Marienplatz

EDUARD MEIER
www.edmeier.de
Munich's oldest shoe

CELEBRATING IN STYLE
When Paul and Elsa Käfer opened a modest food and wine shop in Munich in 1930, they had no idea that their name (▷ 58) would become synonymous with the stylish parties that their son would arrange, in the more prosperous 1960s, for film stars and other prominent members of post-war high society. The shop remains a food-lover's paradise and the catering business supplies such establishments as the roof-top restaurant of the Reichstag (German parliament building) in Berlin.

shop, established in 1596, with leather sofas for ultimate comfort and first-class service.
🔢 J7 ✉ Briennestrasse 22
☎ 22 00 44 🚇 U- or S-Bahn Marienplatz

EILLES-TEE
www.eilles-tee.de
One of several Eilles shops, selling fine tea, coffee and wines.
🔢 J7 ✉ Residenzstrasse 13
☎ 22 61 84 🚇 U- or S-Bahn Marienplatz

ELLY SEIDL
www.ellyseidl.de
A tiny chocolate shop, that is famous for its pralines and its *Münchner Kuppeln* chocolates, which look like the onion-domes of the Frauenkirche.
🔢 J7 ✉ Maffeistrasse 1
☎ 22 44 34 🚇 U- or S-Bahn Marienplatz

FANSHOP
www.fcbayern.de
Everything imaginable to please FC Bayern supporters, from scarves and teddies to clothing and sports bags.
🔢 J7 ✉ Orlandostrasse 1 ☎ 69 93 1666 🚇 U- or S-Bahn Marienplatz

FEINKOST KÄFER
www.feinkost-kaefer.de
An epicurean labyrinth selling food and drink from around the world in the smart Bogenhausen district.
🔢 L7 ✉ Prinzregentenstrasse 73 ☎ 416 8247 🚇 U-Bahn Prinzregentenplatz

HEMMERLE
www.hemmerle.de
The treasures in this traditional Munich jeweler are expensive but beautifully crafted and very solid.
➕ J7 ✉ Maximilianstrasse 14 ☎ 242 2600 🚊 Tram 19

KOKON
www.kokon.com
Here is a magical blend of artifacts, fabrics and furnishings from around the world to suit all tastes. There is an impressive collection of garden furniture and exotic flowers too.
➕ H6 ✉ Lenbach-Palais, Lenbachplatz 3 ☎ 552 5140 🚊 Tram 27

KUNSTGEWERBE-VEREIN
www.kunsthandwerk-bkv.de
Shop here for high-quality, carved, painted and handcrafted Bavarian products. Choose from puppets and pottery to beautiful jewelry and bright carnival masks—truly exclusive gifts.
➕ H7 ✉ Pacellistrasse 6–8 ☎ 290 1470 🚇 U- or S-Bahn Karlsplatz

LODEN-FREY
www.loden-frey.de
Choose your *Trachten* (Bavarian folk costume) from an endless selection here at the world's largest store for national costume. Children will love the toboggan run from the street level to the basement.

➕ J7 ✉ Maffeistrasse 7–9 ☎ 21 03 90 🚇 U- or S-Bahn Marienplatz

LUDWIG BECK BEAUTY
www.ludwigbeck.com
This branch of the Ludwig Beck department store specializes in exotic and extravagant bath and beauty products to pamper the weariest shopper.
➕ J7 ✉ Theatinerstrasse 14, Funf Hof ☎ 23 69 955 🚇 U-Bahn Odeonsplatz

MARKT AM WIENER PLATZ
www.markt-am-wiener-platz.de
Tiny green wooden produce stands huddle around the maypole in Haidhausen—an attractive alternative to the supermarket.
➕ L7 ✉ Wiener Platz 🚇 U-Bahn Max-Weber-Platz

PORZELLAN-MANUFAKTUR NYMPHENBURG
www.nymphenburg.com

This famous porcelain manufacturer still turns out traditional rococo designs. It is based in Nymphenburg Palace, with this outlet in the heart of the city.
➕ J6 ✉ Odeonsplatz 1 ☎ 28 24 28 ⏰ Mon–Fri 10–5 🚇 U-Bahn Odeonsplatz

ROSENTHAL
www.rosenthal.de
Take your choice from the impressive range of smart, contemporary Rosenthal porcelain and glass, together with other choice designer ware.
➕ J7 ✉ Theatinerstrasse 1 ☎ 22 26 17 🚇 U- or S-Bahn Marienplatz

SCHREIBMAYR
www.kaut-bullinger.de
Beautiful desktop equipment, handmade paper and pens for lovers of the dying art of letter writing, together with ink in every imaginable shade, including "King Ludwig's ink."
➕ J7 ✉ Theatinerstrasse 11 (in den Fünf Höfen) ☎ 219 9840 🚇 U- or S-Bahn Marienplatz

THERESA
www.mytheresa.com
Trendy and wildly expensive designer fashions and beautiful accessories, mainly Italian prêt-à-porter, which you'll want to take home.
➕ J7 ✉ Maffeistrasse 3 ☎ 22 48 45 🚇 U-Bahn Odeonsplatz

TRACHTEN AND MORE
The nice thing about *Trachten* (Bavarian folk costume) is that Münchners really do wear it, especially on Sundays, holidays or festive occasions. Most popular are the lederhosen and the smart green-collared grey jackets for men or the brightly coloured dirndl dresses with fitted bodices and full gathered skirts.

Entertainment and Nightlife

CUVILLIÉS-THEATER

www.residenz-muenchen.de
Considered the finest rococo theater in the world, popular for both opera and drama, there is an excellent program of events. Check the website for details
➕ J7 ✉ Residenzstrasse 1 ☎ 29 06 71 🚇 U-Bahn Odeonsplatz

HERKULESSAAL

www.residenz-muenchen.de
Munich's most impressive concert hall, in the Residenz. Check the website for details of forthcoming events.
➕ J7 ✉ Residenzstrasse 1 ☎ 29 06 71 🚇 U-Bahn Odeonsplatz

JAZZCLUB UNTERFAHRT

www.unterfahrt.de
One of Europe's most important jazz clubs featuring modern jazz and avant-garde names.
➕ L7 ✉ Einsteinstrasse 42 ☎ 448 2794 🕐 Sun–Thu 7.30pm–1am, Fri–Sat 7.30pm–3am 🚇 U-Bahn Max-Weber-Platz 🚋 Tram 19

JODLERWIRT

www.jodlerwirt-muenchen.net
This tiny, folksy bar is straight out of the Bavarian countryside—always crowded and jolly, often with local yodelers at night.
➕ J7 ✉ Altenhofstrasse 4 ☎ 22 12 49 🕐 Mon–Sat 7pm–3am 🚇 U- or S-Bahn Marienplatz

KOMÖDIE IM BAYERISCHEN HOF

www.komoedie-muenchen.de
Sophisticated light comedy is the specialty here, while the convivial atmosphere promises a pleasant evening out.
➕ H7 ✉ Promenadeplatz 6 ☎ 2916 1633 🚇 U- or S-Bahn Karlsplatz

MÜNCHNER KAMMERSPIELE

www.muenchner-kammer-spiele.de
The Munich Playhouse is considered one of Germany's best theaters. Tickets are like gold dust so you will need to book well in advance.
➕ J7 ✉ Maximilianstrasse 26–28 ☎ 2333 7100 🚇 U- or S-Bahn Marienplatz

NATIONALTHEATER

www.staatstheater.bayern.de
www.bayerische.staatsoper.de
The home of the Bavarian State Opera (▷ 48) is one of Europe's most

MUSICAL MECCA

Munich and music go hand-in-hand. The city's connection with Mozart, Wagner and Richard Strauss, not to mention its three symphony orchestras, has made it famous throughout the world. Today, it plays host to major events in the musical calendar including the glamorous Opera Festival and the Summer Concert Season at Nymphenburg Palace.

respected opera houses. The excellent opera festival in July is the high point of Munich's cultural year.
➕ J7 ✉ Max-Joseph-Platz ☎ 2185 1920 🚇 U- or S-Bahn Marienplatz

P1

www.p1-club.de
Extremely chic club in the basement of the Haus der Kunst (▷ 52). It has eight different bars frequented by famous faces including models and celebrities.
➕ K6 ✉ Prinzregenten-strasse 1 ☎ 211 1140 🕐 11pm–4am 🚇 U-Bahn Lehel

PRINZREGENTEN-THEATER

www.prinzregententheater. de
Originally built to emulate the famous Wagner Festspielhaus in Bayreuth in 1900. Today it stages a rich program of plays, concerts, opera and musicals.
➕ L7 ✉ Prinzregentenplatz 12 ☎ 2185 2899 🚇 U-Bahn Prinzregentenplatz

SCHUMANN'S

www.schumanns.de
It's hard to get a table here at Germany's number-one bar, but once inside you can enjoy watching Munich's "Schickeria" (chic set) at play.
➕ J6 ✉ Odeonsplatz 6–7 ☎ 22 90 60 🕐 Mon–Fri 5pm–3am, Sun 6pm–3am 🚋 Tram 19

Restaurants

PRICES

Prices are approximate, based on a 3-course meal for one person.

€€€	over €50
€€	€25–€50
€	under €25

BOGENHAUSER HOF (€€€)

www.bogenhauser-hof.de
This small countrified restaurant is located in a picture-book house. Reservations are essential if you wish to sample the inspired French-style cuisine and attentive service.
⊞ L7 ⊠ Ismaninger Strasse 85 ☎ 98 55 86 ◎ Mon–Fri 12–4pm, 6pm–1am 🚋 Tram 18

CAFÉ WIENER PLATZ (€)

www.cafewienerplatz.de
A chic crowd frequents this modern coffeehouse with its extensive breakfast menu.
⊞ L7 ⊠ Innere-Wiener-Strasse 48 ☎ 448 9494 🚋 Tram 19

EISBACH (€€–€€€)

www.eisbach.biz
A chic, modern bar with delicious bagels, pastries, pancakes and freshly squeezed juices served alfresco in summer.
⊞ J7 ⊠ Marstallplatz 3 ☎ 2280 1680 ◎ Daily 10am–1am 🚋 Tram 19

HALALI (€€€)

www.restaurant-halali.de
Halali's secret is good, unpretentious, regional home cooking.
⊞ J6 ⊠ Schönfeldstrasse 22 ☎ 28 59 09 ◎ Mon–Fri lunch, dinner, Sat dinner only 🚇 U-Bahn Odeonsplatz

HAXNBAUER IM SCHOLASTIKAHAUS (€€)

www.kuffler-gastronomie.de
Watch the cooks turning giant shanks of pork (Schweinshax'n) over open beechwood fires in this ancient inn. Huge portions for hungry meat lovers.
⊞ J7 ⊠ Sparkassenstrasse ☎ 216 6540 ◎ Daily 11am–midnight 🚇 U- or S-Bahn Marienplatz

KÄFER-SCHÄNKE (€€€)

www.feinkost-kaefer.de
This warren of rooms above the famous Käfer delicatessen promises a gastronomic experience with creative dishes and a lavish buffet.
⊞ L7 ⊠ Prinzregentenstrasse 73 ☎ 41 68 247

LEBKUCHEN TRADITION

The 600-year-old tradition of baking Lebkuchen is thought to derive from recipes concocted by medieval monks. The biscuits (cookies), are flavored primarily with almonds, honey and spices. The pre-Christmas season is the busiest time for Lebkuchen producer Schmidt when up to 3 million biscuits are made every day.

◎ Mon–Sat 11.30am–1am 🚇 U-Bahn Prinzregentenplatz

KEMPINSKI HOTEL VIER JAHRESZEITEN (€€)

www.kempinski-vierjahreszeiten.com
One of Munich's top hotels serves a traditional English afternoon tea.
⊞ J7 ⊠ Maximilianstrasse 17 ☎ 21 250 ◎ Daily 2–6 🚇 U-Bahn Odeonsplatz 🚋 Tram 19

OSKAR MARIA IM LITERATURHAUS (€€)

www.oskarmaria.com
This airy, modern restaurant attracts an arty set for music and poetry events.
⊞ J6 ⊠ Salvatorplatz 1 ☎ 2919 340 Mon–Sat 10am–12midnight, Sun & holidays 10–7 🚇 U-Bahn Odeonsplatz

SPATENHAUS AN DER OPER (€€)

www.kuffler-gastronomie.de
Top-notch Bavarian cuisine opposite the opera and popular with the after-theater crowd.
⊞ J7 ⊠ Residenzstrasse 12 ☎ 290 7060 ◎ Daily 11.30am–12.30am 🚇 U- or S-Bahn Marienplatz

TRADER VIC'S (€€€)

www.bayerischerhof.de
A varied Polynesian menu ranging from wonton soup to barbecued spare ribs or Calcutta lobster.
⊞ H7 ⊠ Hotel Bayerischer Hof, Promenadeplatz 2–6 ☎ 212 0995 ◎ Daily 5pm–3am 🚇 U- or S-Bahn Marienplatz

Art treasures abound in the tranquil Max suburb, with its many museums and galleries. Trendy Schwabing, beside the Englischer Garten and the university, buzzes with boutiques, bars and restaurants.

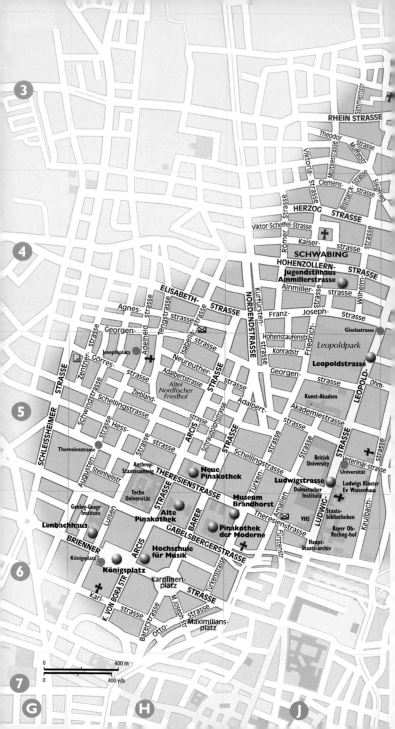

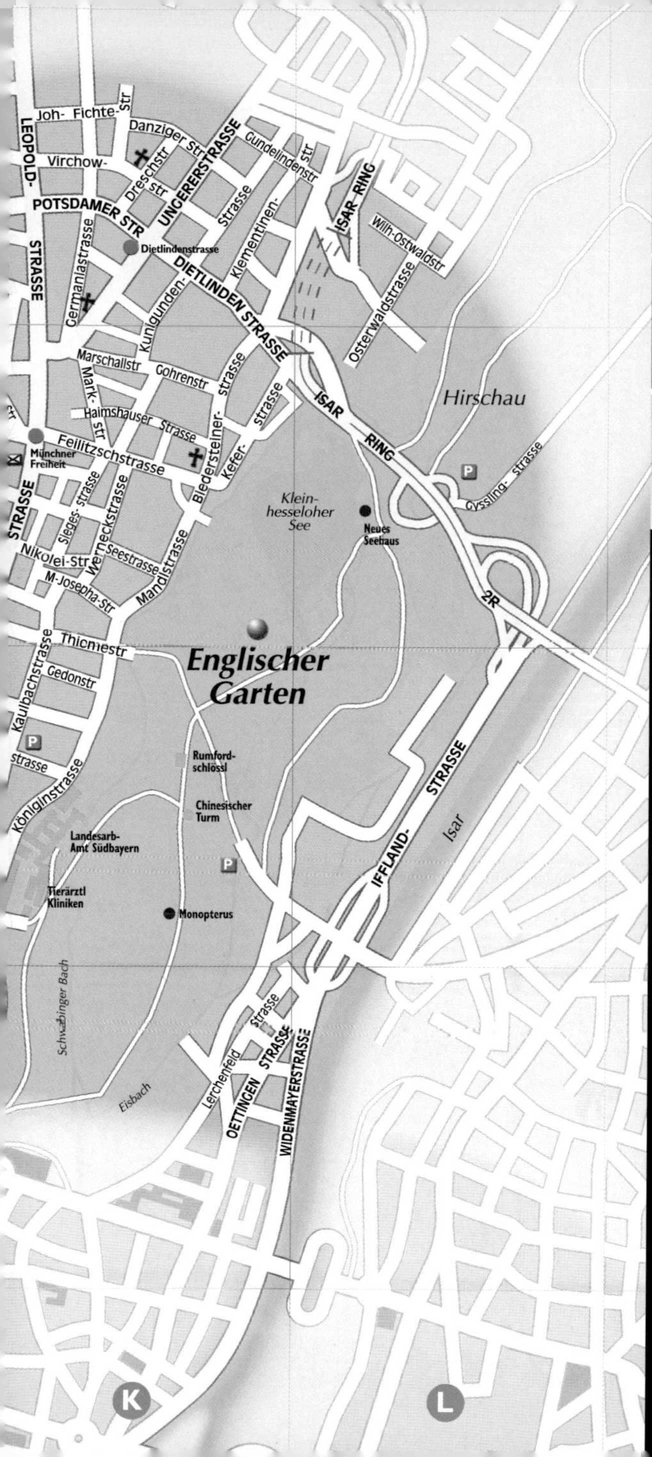

LEOPOLD-

POTSDAMER STR

STRASSE

Joh- Fichte- str

Virchow-

Danziger str

Dreschstr

UNGERERSTRASSE

Gundelindenstr

str

Klementinen-

ISAR- RING

Wilh-Ostwaldstr

Germaniastrasse

Dietlindenstrasse

DIETLINDEN STRASSE

Kunigunden-

strasse

Osterwaldstrasse

Marschallstr

Mark-

Gohrenstr

strasse

Haimshauser Strasse

Kefer-

strasse

ISAR RING

Hirschau

STRASSE

Feilitzschstrasse

Münchner
Freiheit

Biedersteiner-

Klein-
hesseloher
See

Gyssling- strasse

P

Neues
Seehaus

Sieges- strasse

Steckstrasse

Seestrasse

Mandlstrasse

2R

Nikolei-Str

M-Josepha-str

Kaulbachstrasse

Thiemestr

Gedonstr

Englischer
Garten

P

strasse

Königinstrasse

Rumford-
schlössl

IFFLAND-
STRASSE

Isar

Landesarb-
Amt Südbayern

Chinesischer
Turm

P

Tierarztl
Kliniken

Monopterus

Schwabinger Bach

Lerchenfeld
Strasse

OETTINGEN STRASSE

WIDENMAYERSTRASSE

Eisbach

K

L

The Old Masters are the highlight at this art gallery

With more than 850 Old Master paintings, this massive museum, the Old Picture Gallery, is rated alongside the Louvre, Uffizi, Prado and the Metropolitan as one of the world's most important galleries. The Rubens Collection alone is the finest on earth.

Architectural masterpiece The pinnacle of Bavaria's centuries-old dedication to the arts, the gallery was commissioned by Ludwig I and designed by Leo von Klenze to replace the older Kammergalerie in the Residenz, which had become too small for the Royal Collection. Fashioned on the Renaissance palaces of Venice, it took 10 years to construct and on completion in 1836 was proclaimed a masterpiece—the largest gallery building of its time and a model for other museum buildings in Rome and Brussels. During World War II it was so badly damaged that demolition of the site was contemplated. Restored in the 1950s and given an extensive face-lift in the 1990s, the magnificent gallery provides a fitting backdrop for one of the world's finest collections of Western paintings.

Priceless treasures All the main schools of European art from the Middle Ages to the beginning of the 19th century are represented, with the emphasis on German, Dutch and Flemish paintings, including works by Dürer, van Dyck, Rembrandt and Brueghel, and more than 100 pieces by Rubens (the finest collection of its kind in the world).

THE BASICS

www.alte-pinakothek.de
✚ H6
✉ Barer Strasse 27
☎ 23 80 52 16
🕐 Tue 10–8, Wed—Sun 10–6
🚇 U-Bahn Theresienstrasse
🚋 Tram 27
♿ Very good
🖐 Moderate

HIGHLIGHTS

● *Fool's Paradise*, Pieter Brueghel the Elder
● *Four Apostles*, Dürer
● *Adoration of the Magi*, Tiepolo
● *Madonna Tempi*, Raphael
● *The Great Last Judgment*, Rubens
● *The Resurrection*, Rembrandt

Englischer Garten

HIGHLIGHTS

● Chinese Tower
● Kleinhesseloher See and Seehaus
● Monopteros
● Japanese Tea House (tea ceremonies on the second weekend of every month Apr–Oct)
● Rumford House

TIP

● Enjoy a piping-hot cup of *glühwein*, served at the Chinese Tower in winter!

The English Garden ranks highly on every Münchner's list of preferred city spots. On a sunny day, there's nothing more enjoyable than a stroll in this vast, idyllic park, full of people from all walks of life.

Munich's green lung People come here to enjoy themselves – families boating, musicians busking, children feeding the ducks, New Age groups gathered by the love temple, professionals picnicking in their lunch break, jolly crowds in the packed beer gardens. For this is Munich's beloved green lung—373ha (920 acres) of parkland stretching over 5km (3 miles) along the River Isar, and one of the largest city parks in the world.

English influences The English Garden was created by Count Rumford and Ludwig von

The Englischer Garten was Europe's first people's park and is still hugely popular today

Sckell in 1789. Breaking away from the French style of manicured lawns and geometrical flowerbeds, they transformed the Wittelsbach hunting ground into an informal, countrified Volksgarten (people's park).

Attractions Start at the Kleinhesseloher See, an artificial lake with boats for rent. Or spend time relaxing at the Seehaus beer garden before heading south toward the Monopteros, a circular, Greek-style love temple with a splendid view of the park and the distant spires of old Munich. As well as English and Greek influences, the park also has a distinctive oriental tone with its Japanese Tea House and Chinese Tower. It also marks the city's most famous beer garden—popular for its brass band, old-fashioned children's merry-go-round and permanent Oktoberfest atmosphere.

THE BASICS

www.schloesser.bayern.de
➕ K4
🕐 Dawn–dusk
🍴 Chinese Tower beer garden, Seehaus restaurant and beer garden (▷ 78), Japanese Tea House, Aumeister restaurant and beer garden
🚇 U-Bahn Odeonsplatz, Universität, Giselastrasse, Münchner Freiheit
🚌 100, 144, 180, 181, 187, 231, 232; tram 17
❓ Rowing boats for hire at Kleinhesseloher See in summer

Königsplatz

HIGHLIGHTS

Glyptothek
- Barberini Faun
- Mnesarete tomb relief
- Aeginetan marbles
- Boy with a goose

Staatliche Antikensammlung
- Exekias' Dionysus cup
- Golden funerary wreath from Armento

TIP

- There are free guided tours of the museums, on Wednesdays at 6pm for the Staatliche Antikensammlung, and on Thursdays at 6pm for the Glyptothek.

This majestic square, nicknamed "Athens-on-the-Isar," and flanked by three immense neoclassical temples, may come as a surprise in the heart of Munich.

The Square and the Propyläen Along with the buildings of Ludwigstrasse, Königsplatz represents Ludwig I's greatest contribution to Munich. Laid out by Leo von Klenze, according to plans created by Carl von Fischer, the square took 50 years to complete, from 1812 to 1862. The final building, the Propyläen, fashioned after the entrance to the Athenian Acropolis, is the most striking.

Nazi control Between 1933 and 1935, the appearance of Königsplatz was completely transformed. Hitler paved over the grassy, tree-lined

square and Königsplatz became the National Socialists' "Akropolis Germaniae"—a setting for Nazi rallies. The paving stones have been replaced by broad expanses of lawn, enabling Königsplatz to return to its former serenity.

Museums The Glyptothek, or Sculpture Museum, on the north flank of Königsplatz is the oldest museum in Munich and one of the most celebrated neoclassical buildings in Germany. Inside is one of Europe's foremost collections of ancient Greek and Roman sculpture. Look out for the crowned bust of Emperor Augustus and the mosaic terrace depicting Aion from Sentinum. To the south, the Corinthian-style Staatliche Antikensammlung (State Collection of Antiquities) has a priceless collection of ancient vases, jewelry, bronzes and terra-cotta sculptures.

THE BASICS

www.antike-am-koenig-splatz.mwn.de

⊞ H6

✉ Königsplatz

☎ Glyptothek and Antikensammlung 29 92 75 02

🕐 Glyptothek: Tue–Sun 10–5 (Thu until 8); Staatliche Antikensammlung: Tue–Sun 10–5, Wed until 8

🍴 Glyptothek museum café

🚇 U-Bahn Königsplatz

♿ Good (Glyptothek); none (Antikensammlung)

💶 Moderate

Lenbachhaus

Lenbachhaus is a Florentine Renaissance-style villa

THE BASICS

www.lenbachhaus.de

🔲 H6

✉ Luisenstrasse 33

☎ 2333 2000

🕐 Tue 10–9, Wed–Sun 10–6

🍴 Café and garden terrace

🚇 U-Bahn Königsplatz

♿ Good

💷 Moderate

❓ Audio guides are free with admission tickets

HIGHLIGHTS

● Kandinsky collection
● *Der Blaue Reiter* collection
● *Show your Wound,* Joseph Beuys
● *Blue Horse,* Franz Marc
● Munich Jugendstil collection

This beautiful city gallery displays predominantly 19th- and 20th-century works of art. The tiny formal garden is also a delight—a blend of modern and classical statuary and fountains.

The Lenbachhaus This charming villa was built in 1887 in Florentine High Renaissance style by Gabriel von Seidl for the "painter prince" Franz von Lenbach, darling of the German aristocracy and the most fashionable Bavarian painter of his day. After his death, it became the property of the city and was converted into the municipal art gallery (Städtische Galerie im Lenbachhaus). A north wing was added in the late 1920s to balance the south wing, where Lenbach's studio was housed. The resulting structure perfectly frames the terrace and ornamental gardens.

The collections The chief objective of the gallery is to document the development of painting in Munich from the late Gothic period up to the present day. Munich Romantics and landscape artists are well represented, as is the Jugendstil period. However, it is the paintings by the Munich-based expressionist group known as *Der Blaue Reiter* (Blue Rider) that gained the Lenbachhaus international fame. They include over 300 works by Wassily Kandinsky, who founded the movement with Franz Marc. Paul Klee, Gabriele Münter, August Macke and Alexej von Jawlensky are well represented, and the collection of contemporary art by Anselm Kiefer, Andy Warhol, Roy Lichtenstein, Joseph Beuys and others is dazzling.

The New Picture
Gallery was designed
by Alexander von
Branca

Neue Pinakothek

The New Picture Gallery is a shining contrast to the Renaissance-style Old Picture Gallery across the road and carries the art collections on through the 19th and early 20th centuries.

Palazzo Branca As with the Old Picture Gallery (Alte Pinakothek), it was Ludwig I who instigated the building of this gallery as a home for contemporary art in 1846. However, following extensive damage in World War II, a competition was held in 1966 to design a new gallery to be located in the heart of Schwabing, Munich's trendy student quarter.

Successful design The winning entry, by Munich architect Alexander von Branca, opened in 1981. The concrete, granite and glass structure, sometimes known as the Palazzo Branca, integrates art deco and postmodernist designs with traditional features in an unusual figure-of-eight formation around two inner courtyards and terraced ponds.

Art treasures The Neue Pinakothek contains over 1,000 paintings, drawings and sculptures spanning a variety of periods from rococo to Jugendstil, focusing on the development of German art alongside English 19th-century landscapes and portraits, and French Impressionism. It is best to follow the 22 rooms in chronological order, from early Romantic works, then on through French and German late romanticism to French and German Impressionism.

THE BASICS

www.neue-pinakothek.de
+ H5
✉ Barer Strasse 29
☎ 2380 5195
🕐 Wed 10–8, Thu–Mon 10–6
🍽 Café with terrace
🚇 U-Bahn Theresienstrasse
🚋 Tram 27
♿ Very good
💰 Moderate

HIGHLIGHTS

● *Ostende*, William Turner
● *Breakfast*, Edouard Manet
● *Vase with Sunflowers* and *View of Arles*, Vincent van Gogh
● *Large Reclining Woman*, Henry Moore

Pinakothek der Moderne

HIGHLIGHTS

- *World Peace Projected*, Bruce Nauman
- *Madame Soler*, Pablo Picasso
- *The End of the 20th Century*, Joseph Beuys
- *The Starting Line*, with installations by Metzel, Grimonprez, Rist, Dijkstra, Bock and others
- The *Entartete Kunst* (Degenerate Art) collection
- Bauhaus furniture
- Bentwood furniture
- Mobile phone collection

With four major museums under one roof, the Pinakothek der Moderne, founded in 2002, is regarded as one of the world's greatest collections of 20th- and 21st-century art.

State Gallery of Modern Art Half of the total exhibition space in the Pinakothek is occupied by modern art, with an exceptional display of paintings, sculptures, video installations and photographic art, plus incomparable collections of German expressionism and surrealism. Works by Magritte, Picasso, Dalí and Warhol characterize 20th-century art movements, while more recent trends are represented by Rist, Falvin and Wall.

The New Collection This is one of the leading international collections of applied modern arts—

Private sponsors helped to save the Pinakothek der Moderne when the state ran out of money during its construction. It is now the largest museum structure in Europe

a veritable treasure trove of more than 50,000 items (arranged chronologically) illustrating the history of design, with exhibits ranging from cars to computers and from robots to running shoes. Highlights include the avant-garde of the 1920s and 1930s, functionalism, Pop-Art design and the space euphoria of the 1960s.

Architecture Museum The largest collection of its kind in Germany, comprising drawings, photographs and models of more than 700 international architects, displayed in temporary exhibitions examining current trends in German architecture.

State Graphic Art Collection Alongside the Architecture Museum are selections from the State Graphics Collection, which has over 4,000,000 etchings and drawings spanning seven centuries.

THE BASICS

www.pinakothek-der-moderne.de

➕ H6

✉ Barer Strasse 40

☎ 2380 5360

🕐 Tue 10–8, Wed–Sun 10–6

🍴 Café-bistro

Ⓤ U-Bahn Königsplatz or Theresienstrasse

🚌 100; tram 27

♿ Very good

✋ Expensive

❓ Free guided tours

More to See

HOCHSCHULE FÜR MUSIK
www.musikhochschule-muenchen.de
The music academy (formerly Hitler's "Temple of Honor") was designed on Hitler's instruction by Paul Ludwig Troost.
➕ H6 ✉ Arcisstrasse 12 ☎ 2 89 03 Ⓤ U-Bahn Königsplatz

JUGENDSTILHAUS AINMILLERSTRASSE
Munich's first Jugendstil (art nouveau) house (1900) has been restored to its original glory.
➕ J4 ✉ Ainmillerstrasse 22 Ⓤ U-Bahn Giselastrasse

LEOPOLDSTRASSE
The 19th-century Siegestor (a triumphal arch topped with a chariot containing the figure of Bavaria) marks the beginning of the Schwabing district and this fashionable, poplar-lined boulevard. Here you'll find an array of street cafés, fashion boutiques and the wacky *Walking Man* (1995) sculpture by American sculptor Jonathan Borofsky, which is five floors tall.
➕ J5 ✉ Leopoldstrasse Ⓤ U-Bahn Giselastrasse

LUDWIGSTRASSE
This grand avenue, which continues into Leopoldstrasse, was laid out by Ludwig I. It contains Peter Cornelius's *Last Judgment*, the second largest fresco in the world (after Michaelangelo's *Last Judgment* in the Sistine Chapel, Rome), which took four years to complete.
➕ J5 ✉ Ludwigstrasse Ⓤ U-Bahn Odeonsplatz, Universität

MUSEUM BRANDHORST
www.museum-brandhorst.de
This museum houses the Brandhorst Collection of modern art. Highlights include illustrated books by Picasso, large collections of Warhol and Cy Twombly, and important works by Polke, Beuys, Nauman and Hirst. The museum also has a growing collection of multi-media installations.
➕ J6 ✉ Theresienstrasse 35a ☎ 2380 5104 Ⓤ U-Bahn Königsplatz, Theresienstrasse 🚌 100; tram 27

Walking Man *on Leopoldstrasse*

Jugendstilhaus

Galleries and Gardens

From the world-class art galleries via Schwabing's trendy bars and boutiques to the Englischer Garten, this walk appeals to everyone.

DISTANCE: 1.8km (1.1 miles) **ALLOW:** 2.5 hours (excluding visits)

START

KÖNIGSPLATZ (▷ 66)
✛ H6 🚇 Königsplatz

END

ENGLISCHER GARTEN (▷ 64–65)
✛ L4 🚇 Münchner Freiheit

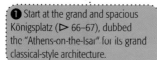

1 Start at the grand and spacious Königsplatz (▷ 66–67), dubbed the "Athens-on-the-Isar" for its grand classical-style architecture.

2 Here you will find yourself surrounded by museums: choose from the gallery in Lenbachhaus (▷ 68), the Glyptothek (▷ 67) and the Staatliche Antikensammlung (▷ 67).

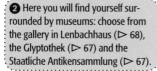

3 Proceed along Briennerstrasse, and turn left into Barer Strasse at the obelisk in Karolinenplatz. This is the heart of the city's Kunstareal (art district), and the surrounding streets are brimming with small private galleries.

4 Before long you will pass by three of its most important galleries: the Alte Pinakothek (▷ 62–63); Neue Pinakothek (▷ 69); and Pinakothek der Moderne (▷ 70–71).

8 While away the hours in the English Garden, then head northwards to the boating lake and neighboring Seehaus beer garden (▷ 78).

7 The university is marked by two fountains. A right turn here will lead you along Veterinärstrasse and into the city's vast green space, the Englischer Garten (▷ 64–65). The Chinese Tower nearby is the site of Munich's most popular beer garden.

6 The end of Schellingstrasse is marked by the Ludwigskirche, which contains one of the world's largest frescoes. Turn left here into Ludwigstrasse (▷ 72), a grand avenue laid out by Ludwig I.

5 Continue up Barer Strasse then turn right along Schellingstrasse, just one of the maze of streets behind the university, bursting with student life.

Shopping

2-RAD
www.2rad-schwabing.de
This shop has everything a bicycle fanatic could possibly want.
🕀 J4 ✉ Georgenstrasse 39 ☎ 271 6383 🚊 Tram 27

LE CHALET DU FROMAGE
One of Munich's best cheesemongers.
🕀 J4 ✉ Stand 11, Elisabethplatz ☎ 271 2243 🕐 Closed Mon 🚊 Tram 27

CHINA'S WORLD
www.chinasworld.de
This specialist shop sells antique Rosenthal porcelain.
🕀 J5 ✉ Kurfürstenstrasse 15 ☎ 2738 9900 🚇 U-Bahn Universität, Giselastrasse

ELISABETHMARKT
Schwabing's answer to the Viktualienmarkt, and with surprisingly few tourists to spoil the ambience.
🕀 J4 ✉ Elisabethplatz 🚊 Tram 27

FLIP
www.flipmunich.de
Stocks an impressive range of name labels specializing in cool ready-to-wear fashion and footwear for both men and women.
🕀 K4 ✉ Feilitzschstrasse 4 ☎ 3808 8659 🚇 U-Bahn Münchner Freiheit

HALLHUBER
www.hallhuber.de
Leading labels at very reasonable prices;

popular with trendy young shoppers.
🕀 J7 ✉ Marienplatz 17 ☎ 260 8412 🚇 U- or S-Bahn Marienplatz

KINDER-AMBIENTE
www.kinder-ambiente.de
Beautiful toys, fittings and furnishings to create the perfect children's bedroom.
🕀 G5 ✉ Schleissheimer-strasse 73 ☎ 1433 0230 🚇 U-Bahn Josephsplatz

KREMER PIGMENTE
www.kremer-pigmente.com
A tiny shop opposite the Neue Pinakothek selling more than 500 different shades for artists in every medium from oils to watercolors, together with paper and brushes.
🕀 H6 ✉ Barer Strasse 46 ☎ 28 54 88 🚊 Tram 27

KUNST UND SPIEL
www.kunstundspiel.de
A magical shop full of sturdy, educational toys

TOYS
Germany has been one of the world's leading toy manufacturers since the Middle Ages, and is particularly famous for its china dolls, tin-plate toys and Steiff teddy bears. Many important manufacturing areas are around Munich—Nuremberg, Oberammergau and Berchtesgaden. Today, old Steiff bears are considered great collector's pieces.

together with an extensive arts and craft section.
🕀 K4 ✉ Leopoldstrasse 48 ☎ 381 6270 🚇 U-Bahn Giselastrasse

LANDPARTIE
A warm country atmosphere welcomes you into this homely shop, crammed with antique furniture and household accessories.
🕀 J5 ✉ Kurfürstenstrasse 10-12 ☎ 34 85 98 🚊 Tram 27

PERLENMARKT
www.perlenmarkt.de
This unusual shop sells nothing but buttons, beads and jewelry-making equipment.
🕀 J5 ✉ Nordendstrasse 28 ☎ 271 0576 🚊 Tram 27

DIE PUPPENSTUBE
Dolls and puppets to take you back to your childhood.
🕀 H5 ✉ Luisenstrasse 68 ☎ 272 3267 🚊 53

STOCKHAMMER
Idea-hungry shoppers are sure to find original gifts for all ages here.
🕀 J4 ✉ Hohenzollernstrasse 33 ☎ 34 77 81 🚇 U- or S-Bahn Münchner Freiheit

WORDS' WORTH
www.wordsworth.de
Anglophiles will find a large range of English books here, as well as a Pooh Corner for children and a National Trust shop.
🕀 J5 ✉ Schellingstrasse 3 ☎ 280 9141 🚊 53

Entertainment and Nightlife

side margin: MAXVORSTADT AND SCHWABING ENTERTAINMENT AND NIGHTLIFE

ALTE GALERIE
www.alte-galerie.de
A youthful dance club and bar, in a cellar that trades Schwabing chic for genuine atmosphere and an eclectic range of music.
K5 ⊠ Kaulbachstrasse 75 ☎ 34 98 87 🕔 Daily from 8pm 🚇 U-Bahn Giselastrasse

ARRI KINO
www.arri-kino.de
One of Munich's main arthouse cinemas with a rich program and broad audience appeal.
J5 ⊠ Türkenstrasse 91 ☎ 3889 9664 🚇 U-Bahn Universität

HOCHSCHULE FÜR MUSIK
www.musikhochschule-muenchen.de
Young up-and-coming musicians from the Music Academy give regular free evening concerts and lunchtime recitals. Call for details of forthcoming events.
H6 ⊠ Arcisstrasse 12 ☎ 28903 🚇 U-Bahn Königsplatz

LACH- UND SCHIESS-GESELLSCHAFT
www.lachundschiess.de
Germany's most satirical revues are performed here; while the convivial and comfortable atmosphere makes for a relaxing evening.
K4 ⊠ Haimhauser-Ursulastrasse ☎ 39 19 97 🚇 U-Bahn Münchner Freiheit

MARIONETTEN-THEATER KLEINES SPIEL
www.kleinesspiel.de
Puppet shows for adults, with a repertoire of productions by such writers as Bertolt Brecht, Ludwig Thoma and Ben Jonson. Performances Thursday at 8pm. Free, but there's a box for donations by the door.
H5 ⊠ Neureutherstrasse 12 ☎ 272 3364 🚋 Tram 27

MÜNCHNER SOMMERTHEATER
www.muenchner-sommertheater.de
Each July the Munich Summer Theater presents a series of popular open-air performances in

BEER GARDENS
The Bavarian capital city's renowned beer gardens thrive from the first warm days of spring to the annual drinking climax of the *Oktoberfest* (▷ 92), when they are augmented by huge party tents erected on a city meadow (Theresienwiese, ▷ 88). Before electrical refrigeration was invented, brewers planted chestnut trees above their storage cellars to help keep supplies cool, then put out tables and benches in the shade to welcome drinkers. To this day, the spring-flowering of the chestnut trees heralds the start of the beer garden season.

the Englischer Garten's amphitheater.
K5 ⊠ Rümelinstrasse 8 ☎ 98 93 88 🚇 U-Bahn Alte Heide 🚌 Bus 187

ROXY
www.caferoxy.de
A popular place to see and be seen. Great for people-watching.
K4 ⊠ Leopoldstrasse 48 ☎ 34 92 92 🕔 8am–3am 🚇 U-Bahn Giselastrasse

SCHWABINGER PODIUM
www.schwabinger-podium.com
A small, popular venue that does rock'n'roll and blues.
K4 ⊠ Wagnerstrasse 1 ☎ 39 94 82 🕔 Mon–Fri 8pm–1am, Sat–Sun 8pm–3am 🚇 U-Bahn Münchner Freiheit

THEATER BEI HEPPEL & ETTLICH
www.heppel-ettlich.de
A relaxed atmosphere and a glass of beer welcome you to this student bar-cum-theater.
K4 ⊠ Feilitzstrasse 12 ☎ 3888 7820 🚉 S-Bahn Münchner Freiheit

THEATER DER JUGEND
www.schauburg.net
The shows put on here are designed to appeal to both small children (morning and afternoon performances) and teenagers (evening).
J4 ⊠ Schauburg, Franz-Joseph-Strasse 47 ☎ 2333 7155 🚇 U-Bahn Giselastrasse

Restaurants

PRICES

Prices are approximate, based on a 3-course meal for one person.

€€€	over €50
€€€	€25–€50
€	under €25

BACHMAIER HOFBRÄU (€)

www.bachmaier-hofbraeu.de
The menu at this comfy bar-restaurant goes beyond the expected Bavarian standbys, to take in a few continental dishes, and weekend brunch.

➕ K4 ✉ Leopoldstrasse 50 ☎ 3838 680 🕐 Mon–Thu 11am–1am, Fri 11am–3am, Sat 10am–3am, Sun 10am–1am 🚇 Giselastrasse

CAFÉ ALTSCHWABING (€)

www.altschwabing.com
Enjoy a leisurely breakfast in this elegant café with tasteful Jugendstil decor and well-cooked food.

➕ H5 ✉ Schellingstrasse 56 ☎ 273 1022 🕐 Daily 9am–1am 🚌 53; tram 27

CAFÉ IGNAZ (€)

www.ignaz-cafe.de
A vegan and vegetarian café with a large pleasant terrace and friendly staff, serving some of the best vegetarian pizzas and risotto in town.

➕ H5 ✉ Georgenstrasse 67 ☎ 271 6093 🕐 Mon, Wed– Fri 8am–10pm, Tue 11–10, Sat, Sun 9am–10pm 🚇 U-Bahn Josephsplatz

CAFÉ PUCK (€)

www.cafepuck.de
A spacious, trendy student haunt in Schwabing. Excellent for breakfast.

➕ J5 ✉ Türkenstrasse 33 ☎ 280 2280 🕐 Daily 9am–1am 🚇 U-Bahn Universität

CAFÉ REITSCHULE (€€)

www.cafe-reitschule.de
Watch the horses practise as you eat in the historic Riding School, or enjoy breakfast on the terrace overlooking the English Garden.

SECOND BREAKFAST

With such a thriving café scene, taking breakfast in Munich is very popular. There are even a couple of home-delivery breakfast services in town. And, as many people in Munich start their working day very early, they often indulge in a mid-morning snack to bridge the gap between breakfast and lunch, called *Brotzeit* (bread time). This may be a sandwich or the traditional local specialty of boiled *Weisswürste* (white sausages) and *Brezen* (pretzels, knotted rolls sprinkled with coarse grains of salt). There are plenty of opportunities to indulge in *Brotzeit*, whether working on-the-move from a street stall or relaxing in a shady beer garden.

➕ K5 ✉ Königinstrasse 34 ☎ 388 8780 🕐 Daily 9am–1am 🚇 U-Bahn Giselastrasse

LE CÉZANNE (€€€)

www.le-cezanne.de
This tiny bistro special- izes in delicious Provençal fare.

➕ J5 ✉ Konradstrasse 1 ☎ 39 18 05 🕐 Tue–Sun evenings only 🚇 U-Bahn Giselastrasse

GRISSINI (€€)

www.grissini.com
An excellent Italian restaurant, decorated like an Italian palazzo; the service is good too.

➕ K3 ✉ Helmtrudenstrasse 1 ☎ 3610 1213 🕐 Lunch, dinner; closed Sat lunch 🚇 U-Bahn Dietlindenstrasse

HUCKEBEIN ESSEN & WEIN (€€€)

www.huckebein.com
Jan Rubbenshroth's stylish but relaxed atmosphere is a great setting for the seasonal menu based on local produce.

➕ J5 ✉ Amalienstrasse 89 ☎ 5480 4679 🕐 Mon–Fri 12–2.30, 6–10.30, Sat 6–10.30 🚇 U-Bahn Universität

MAX EMANUEL BRÄUEREI (€)

www.max-emanuel-brauerei.de
This tiny, crowded beer garden is known for its folk music and its con- vivial atmosphere.

➕ J5 ✉ Adalbertstrasse 33 ☎ 271 5158 🕐 Daily 11–11 (evenings only in winter) 🚇 U-Bahn Universität

MAXVORSTADT AND SCHWABING RESTAURANTS

NEWS BAR (€)

www.newsbarmunich.de
Catch up on the news over breakfast with a selection of international newspapers and magazines.
➕ J5 ✉ Amalienstrasse 55 ☎ 28 17 87 🕙 Daily 7.30am–2am 🚇 U-Bahn Universität

OSTERIA (€€€)

www.osteria.de
Top-notch Italian cuisine in beautiful surroundings. A venerable villa.
➕ H5 ✉ Schellingstrasse 62 ☎ 272 0717 🕙 Mon–Sat lunch, dinner 🚌 53

RILANO NO. 6 (€€€)

www.rilano-no6.com
Located in the imposing Lenbach Palais this stylish restaurant is popular with locals and visitors alike.
➕ H6 ✉ Ottostrasse 6 ☎ 5491 300 🕙 Lunch, dinner; closed Sun 🚇 U-or S-Bahn Karlsplatz

ROSSO PIZZA (€)

Order a takeout pizza here to enjoy in the Englischer Garten, just a two-minute walk away.
➕ J5 ✉ Amalienstrasse 45 ☎ 2737 5653 🕙 Mon–Sat 8am–10pm 🚇 U-Bahn Universität

SAUSALITO'S (€€)

www.sausalitos.de
A fun, vibrant Tex-Mex restaurant with a lively party atmosphere and sensational margarita cocktails.
➕ J6 ✉ Türkenstrasse 50 ☎ 28 15 94 🕙 Sun–Thu

5pm–1am, Fri, Sat 5pm–3am
🚇 U-Bahn Universität

SCHELLING SALON (€–€€)

For over 140 years this famous Munich café has served Leberkäse, Knödel and other traditional fare. Also has a billiard room.
➕ H5 ✉ Schellingstrasse 34 ☎ 2720 788 🕙 Mon, Thu–Sun 10–1am 🚇 U-Bahn Universität

SEEHAUS IM ENGLIS-CHEN GARTEN (€€)

www.kuffler-gastronomie.de
Popular beer garden at the heart of the English Garden, overlooking the boating lake.
➕ L4 ✉ Kleinhesselohe 3 ☎ 38 16 130 🕙 10am–1am 🚇 U-Bahn Münchner Freiheit

SEOUL (€€)

One of Munich's few Korean restaurants is in the heart of Schwabing.
➕ K4 ✉ Leopoldstrasse 122 ☎ 34 8104 🕙 Lunch, dinner; closed 1st, 3rd Mon of month 🚇 U-Bahn Münchner Freiheit

VEGETARIAN SURPRISE

Think of Bavarian cuisine and many people conjure up images of enormous joints of meat and miles of sausages. However, Munich offers some excellent vegetarian restaurants. Their menus are particularly interesting during *Spargelzeit* (Asparagus Season) in May and June when asparagus is served in an amazing variety of ways.

LA STELLA (€€)

Terrific pizzas draw a young crowd to this excellent trattoria.
➕ J5 ✉ Hohenstaufenstrasse 2 ☎ 34 17 79 🕙 Lunch, dinner 🚇 U-Bahn Giselastrasse

TANTRIS (€€€)

www.tantris.de
Munich's top restaurant, with top chef Hans Haas, is renowned for its excellent service and contemporary cuisine.
➕ K3 ✉ Johann-Fichte-Strasse 7 ☎ 361 9590 🕙 Tue–Sat lunch, dinner 🚇 U-Bahn Dietlindenstrasse

TIRAMISU (€)

Tiny Italian bar serving excellent antipasti. Daily changing pasta menu.
➕ J4 ✉ Hohenzollernstrasse 124 ☎ 308 6008 🕙 Mon–Fri 11.30–10, Sat 11.30–5 🚇 U-Bahn Hohenzollernplatz

TRESZNJEWSKI (€€)

www.tresznjewski.de
This trendy brasserie, opposite the Neue Pinakothek (▷ 69), is packed with diners from breakfast until the early hours.
➕ H5 ✉ Theresienstrasse 72 ☎ 28 23 49 🕙 Daily 8am–3am 🚋 Tram 27

VINI E PANINI (€)

Bread, wine and delicious snacks from different regions of Italy.
➕ J4 ✉ Nordendstrasse 45 ☎ 272 1743 🕙 Mon–Fri 10–6.30, Sat 8–2 🚋 Tram 27

West Munich

There's plenty to see in Munich's western suburbs, from the high-tech world of BMW and the Olympiapark to Germany's finest baroque palace at Nymphenburg.

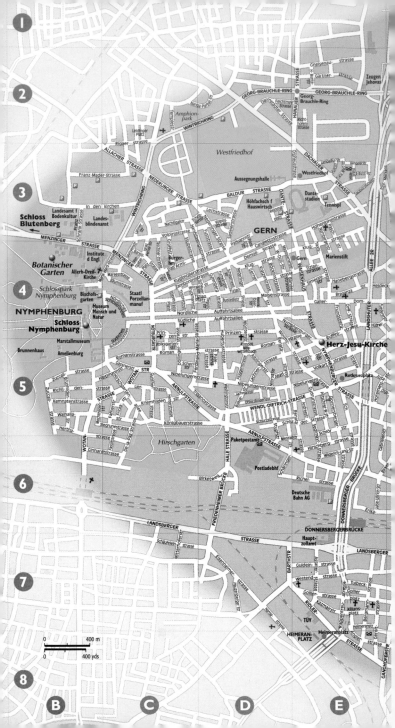

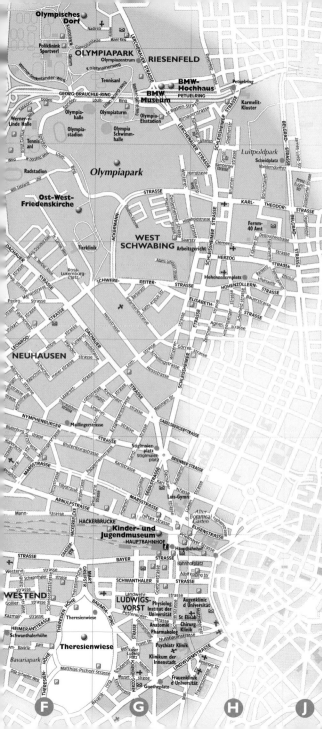

Olympisches Dorf

Poliklinik Sportverl

OLYMPIAPARK

RIESENFELD

Olympiazentrum

BMW-Hochhaus

BMW Museum

PETUELRING

Petuelring

Karmelit-Kloster

Tennisanl

GEORG-BRAUCHLE-RING

Werner-Linde Halle

Olympia-halle

Olympiaturm

Olympia-Eisstadion

Luitpoldpark

Scheidplatz

Olympia-stadion

Olympia Schwimm-halle

Radstadion

Olympiapark

KARL- THEODOR- STRASSE

Ost-West-Friedenskirche

Fernm-40 Amt

Tierklinik

WEST SCHWABING

Rosa-Luxemburg-Platz

Arbeitsgericht

HERZOG

Hohenzollernplatz

HOHENZOLLERN- STRASSE

Bauerstrasse

Pedro strasse

ELISABETH-

LEONROD

NEUHAUSEN

Maillingerstrasse

NYMPHENBURGER

Stiglmaier platz
Stiglmaier platz

BRIENNER STRASSE

MARSSTRASSE

Karlstrasse

ARNULFSTRASSE

Luis-Gymn

After Botanical Garten

HACKERBRUCKE

Kinder- und Jugendmuseum

ELISENSTRASSE

HAUPTBAHNHOF

Hauptbahnhof

STRASSE

BAYER

Bahnhofplatz

SCHWANTHALER

STRASSE

WESTEND

Augenklinik d Universität

LUDWIGS-VORST

Physiolog Institut der Universität

St Elisab

Heimeranstr

Anatomie

Chirur Klinik

Schwanthalerhöhe

BAVARIA-RING

Pharmakolog

Nussbaumstrasse

Bavariapark

Theresienwiese

Psychiatr Klinik

Klinikum der Innenstadt

Frauenklinik d Universität

Matthias-Pschorr-strasse

Goetheplatz

F G H J

Olympiapark

DID YOU KNOW?

● The Olympic Park covers more than 3sq km (1sq mile)
● The Olympiaturm is 290m (950ft) high
● The Olympic Stadium holds 63,000 people
● The Olympic Village houses about 9,000 people

TIPS

● The stadium roof climb tour also offers abseiling.
● Children will love the sealife aquarium.

Since the 1972 Olympics the park, with its intriguing skyline, has become one of the city's landmarks. Its tower offers an unforgettable view of Munich and the Alps.

The Games The historic Oberwiesenfeld was a former royal Bavarian parade ground north of the city. In 1909 the world's first airship landed here, and from 1925 until 1939 it was Munich's airport. Used as a dump during World War II, it was transformed in 1968 into a multifunctional sport and recreation area. In 1972 it was the site of the 20th Summer Olympic Games.

The buildings The television tower here, now called the Olympiaturm, built between 1965 and 1968, is the tallest reinforced concrete

Olympiapark was built for the Summer Olympics in 1972. The viewing platform of the Olympiaturm (Olympic Tower) at 190m (623ft) offers stunning panoramas

construction in Europe, and has become a symbol of modern Munich. When the weather is clear, the viewing platform and revolving restaurant give a breathtaking panorama of the Alps; the view of the city at night is magical. The stadium's futuristic tent-roof looks like an immense spider's web. When you tour the area on a little train you will see the Olympiasee, a huge artificial lake; the Olympiaberg, a 53m (174ft) hill constructed from wartime rubble; the quaint Russian Orthodox chapel built by Father Timofej, a Russian recluse, beautifully decorated inside with thousands of pieces of silver paper (▷ 88); and the Olympic Village (▷ 87), remembered sadly today as the scene of the terrorist attack on 5 September 1972, in which 11 Israeli athletes and coaches and a German police officer were killed.

THE BASICS

www.olympiapark-muenchen.de

✚ G3

✉ Spiridon-Louis-Ring 21

☎ 30 67 0

🕐 Olympiaturm daily 9–midnight. Olympiastadion mid-Apr to mid-Oct daily 8.30–8.30; mid-Oct to mid-Apr 9–4.30

🍴 Revolving restaurant

Ⓤ U-Bahn Olympiazentrum

🚌 173, 177, 178; tram 20, 21

Schloss Nymphenburg

TOP 25

HIGHLIGHTS

- Amalienburg
- Badenburg
- Gallery of Beauties
- Porcelain Museum
- Magdalenenklause
- Marstallmuseum
- Botanical Garden (▷ 87)

TIPS

- On weekends, the gardens are especially popular.
- Be sure to visit the Badenburg, said to be Europe's first post-Roman heated pool.

It is hard to believe that one of Germany's largest baroque palaces, set in magnificent parkland, started life as a modest summer villa. This is one of Munich's loveliest areas.

The palace Five generations of Bavarian royalty were involved in the construction of this vast palace, starting with Elector Ferdinand Maria. Thrilled by the birth of his heir Max Emanuel, he had the central section built for his wife, Henriette Adelaide of Savoy, commissioning an Italian-style villa by Agostino Barelli in 1664. The villa was completed 10 years later. However, starting with Max Emanuel, each succeeding ruler added to the building, resulting in a majestic, semicircular construction, stretching 500m (550yds) from one wing to the other.

The interior The central structure contains sumptuous galleries, including Ludwig I's Gallery of Beauties, featuring 36 Munich ladies, some said to have been the king's mistresses. In the old stables, the Marstallmuseum's dazzling collection of state carriages and sleighs recalls the heyday of the Wittelsbach family. The Porcelain Museum provides a comprehensive history of the famous Nymphenburg porcelain factory (▷ 90) since its foundation in 1747.

Park and pavilions Originally in Italian then French baroque style, the gardens were transformed in 1803 into a fashionable English park with ornate waterways, statues, pavilions and a maze. See yourself reflected 10-fold in the Hall of Mirrors in the Amalienburg hunting lodge and visit the shell-encrusted Magdalenenklause hermitage.

THE BASICS

www.schloss-nymphen-burg.de

➕ B4

☎ 17 90 80

🕐 Palace Apr–mid-Oct daily 9–6; mid-Oct–Mar daily 10–4. Park Jan, Feb, Nov 6.30–6, Mar 6am–6.30pm; Apr, Sep 6–8.30; May–Aug 6am–9.30, Oct 6.30am–7pm

🍴 Café Palmenhaus

🚇 U-Bahn Rotkreuzplatz

🚌 51; tram 12, 16, 17

♿ None

💷 Moderate

BMW Museum

THE BASICS

www.bmw-museum.de
➕ G2
✉ Am Olympiapark 2
(Petuelring)
☎ 1250 16001
🕐 Tue–Sun 10–6
🚇 U-Bahn
Olympiazentrum
🚌 36, 41, 43, 81, 136, 184
♿ Excellent
💰 Expensive
❓ Phone in advance for a
factory tour

HIGHLIGHTS

● 1899 Wartburg Motor
Wagon
● 1923 R32 motorcycle
● 1931 Cabriolet
● 1934 Roadster
● 1936 BMW 328
● 1952 The Baroque Angel
(BMW 501)
● 1955 BMW 507 roadster
● 2014 H2R Hydrogen car

Even if the world of automobiles doesn't particularly interest you, it's hard not to marvel at the developments of transport technology over the past five generations presented at the most popular company museum in Germany.

The museum The BMW Time Horizon Museum, housed in a half sphere, provides an eye-catching contrast to the adjacent high-rise headquarters of BMW (▷ 87). Over a quarter of a million visitors come to the BMW Museum annually to see its rare cars and motorcycles. As well as vintage BMW models, there are also insights into the past through slides and videos covering such subjects as changing family life and work conditions, the role of women in industry and car recycling (where BMW is at the forefront of development).

Future vision Take a simulated journey into the future with electric or solar-generated hydrogen-drive cars or design your own model and watch it develop on computers. Adults and children vie with each other to sit in the cockpit of tomorrow's car and experiment with its sophisticated data and information systems. At the museum's cinema, a film *Das weisse Phantom* (The White Phantom) about motorcycle race world champion Ernst Jakob Henne brings the world of motor-racing to life. Just across Lerchenauer Strasse is the futuristic BMW Welt (World) building, where car buyers can take delivery direct from the factory.

More to See

BMW-HOCHHAUS

This giant, silver, four-cylinder building resembles a four-leaf clover. The company's headquarters was built between 1970 and 1972 to a design by Viennese architect Karl Schwanzer to signal BMW's company's technical orientation.

➕ G2 ✉ Petuelring 130 🚇 U-Bahn Petuelring

BOTANISCHER GARTEN

www.botmuc.de

The Botanical Garden lies at the northern end of the Nymphenburger Park (▷ 84–85) and attracts visitors to its outdoor gardens and greenhouses over 20ha (50 acres). The best time to see the gardens in full bloom is in May and June.

➕ B4 ✉ Menzinger Strasse 65 ☎ 17861 310 🕓 Nov–Jan daily 9–4.30; Feb–Mar, Oct 9–5; Apr–Sep 9–6; May–Aug 9–7 🍴 Café 🚋 Tram 17 💷 Inexpensive

HERZ-JESU-KIRCHE

www.herzjesu-muenchen.de

The Heart of Jesus Church was completely rebuilt after a fire destroyed the old church in 1994. The new architectural wonder lays claim to the largest church doors in the world, while the facade is covered in glass panels. On the portal wings the Passion of Christ is depicted in a series of iconographical images.

➕ E5 ✉ Lachnerstrasse 8 ☎ 130 6750 🕓 Daily 8–8 🚇 U-Bahn Rotkreuzplatz 🖐 Free

KINDER- UND JUGENDMUSEUM

www.kindermuseum-muenchen.de

There is a wide variety of hands-on activities and exhibitions that will delight children and young people in this museum, which aims to promote active learning and awaken curiosity.

➕ G6 ✉ Arnulfstrasse 3 ☎ 540 46440 🕓 Tue–Fri 2–5.30, Sat, Sun 11–5.30 🚇 Hauptbahnhof 💷 Moderate

OLYMPISCHES DORF

During the Summer Olympics of 1972, athletes from around the world stayed in the apartments and

Botanischer Garten at the north end of the Nymphenburger Park

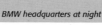

BMW headquarters at night

bungalows here in the Olympic Village. Now most are privately owned or occupied by students.
🔲 F1 🚇 U-Bahn Olympiazentrum

OST-WEST-FRIEDENSKIRCHE
This unusual Russian Orthodox church was made from refuse, such as tin cans and sweet wrappers, by the Russian hermit Father Timofej, who lived here for decades before he died in 2004. When ordered to leave to make way for the Olympic riding stadium, he protested with the help of some Munich citizens and the stadium was constructed elsewhere.
🔲 F3 🚇 U-Bahn Olympiazentrum

SCHLOSS BLUTENBURG
www.blutenburg.de
A moated 15th-century castle in Obermenzing. The romantic Schloss Blutenburg was originally built as a love-nest for Agnes Bernauer by her secret lover, Duke Albrecht III, in 1438. Sadly, shortly after completion of the magical castle, she was accused of being a witch and was

drowned in the Danube at Straubing. This one-time Wittelsbach summer residence contains an international collection of children's books—the largest library of youth literature in the world, with more than 500,000 in 100 different languages.
🔲 Off map to west ✉ Seldweg 15, Obermenzing ☎ 17 90 80 🕐 Chapel daily Apr–Sep 9–5; Oct–Mar 10–4. Library Mon–Fri 2pm–6pm 🚇 S-Bahn Obermenzing
🎫 Free admission to chapel

THERESIENWIESE
"Theresa's fields" are best known as the venue for the world's biggest beer festival—the Oktoberfest, with its hefty beermaids serving the heaving throng. It all began in 1810 with the wedding party of Crown Prince Ludwig and Princess Theresa—a lavish affair with horse racing, shooting matches and a fair but, ironically, no beer. Here too is the 18m (60ft) high Statue of Bavaria; climb the 112 steps inside for great city views.
🔲 F8 ✉ Theresienwiese 🚇 U-Bahn Theresienwiese

Schloss Blutenburg

Oktoberfest at Theresienwiese

Green Munich

Escape the bustling city center and visit Schloss Nymphenburg and its gardens, followed by a canal-side stroll to the Olympiapark.

DISTANCE: 3.5km (2.2 miles) **ALLOW:** all day (including visits)

START

ROTKREUZPLATZ
✚ E5 🚇 U-Bahn Rotkreuzplatz

END

OLYMPIAPARK (▷ 82–83)
✚ G3 🚇 U-Bahn Olympiapark

① Start at Rotkreuzplatz, and head northwards up Nymphenburger-strasse. After a short distance, turn left down Lachnerstrasse past the Herz-Jesu-Kirche (▷ 87).

⑧ From here, it is a 2.5km (1.5 mile) walk through quiet, green suburbs, following the course of the canal all the way to the Olympiapark (▷ 82–83).

② Just past the church, turn right into Winthirstrasse. At the junction with Romanstrasse, note the ornamental Jugendstil (art nouveau) façade at No. 5 (to your right).

⑦ Return to the canal via the Nordliche Schlossrondell, past the famous Porzellan-Manufaktur Nymphenburg. At Ludwig-Ferdinand-Brücke, turn left onto Menzingerstrasse. Cross the road and take a narrow right turn up Kuglmüller-strasse immediately after the tiny Nymphenburg canal.

③ Continue up Winthirstrasse past some of the grand mansions of this leafy, exclusive residential area until you reach the canal.

⑥ The vast palace was constructed by five consecutive generations of Bavarian royalty, and contains several museums and galleries. The Porcelain Museum here provides a history of the famous porcelain factory (▷ 90).

④ Turn left and stroll along the banks of the canal, along the Südliche Auffahrtsallee. During very cold winters, locals can be seen ice-skating on the canal.

⑤ Eventually you will reach Schloss Nymphenburg (▷ 84–85).

Shopping

ANGERMAIER
www.trachten-angermaier.de
Quality traditional German costumes and accessories for men and women.
⊞ E7 ⊠ Landsburgerstrasse 101 ☎ 501677 🚇 S-Bahn Donnersbergerbrücke

L'ANTIPASTO
www.lantipasto.de
A small, friendly Italian delicatessen selling mouth-watering antipasti, fresh pasta, sauces, wines and condiments—the perfect place to pick up a picnic.
⊞ F5 ⊠ Sanstrasse 33 ☎ 5230 0824 🚇 U-Bahn Stiglmaierplatz

ARMIN'S RÄUCHERKUCHL
www.armins-raucherkuchl.de
A tiny, traditional Tirolean-style delicatessen, serving salamis, cold cuts and fine regional wines.
⊞ E5 ⊠ Blutenburgstrasse 55 ☎ 12 92 123 🚇 U-Bahn Rotkreuzplatz

BUBE & DAME
www.bube-dame.com
Excellent range of well-priced fashion for men and women. Friendly, helpful service.
⊞ E6 ⊠ Wilderich-Lang-Strasse 6 ☎ 3853 4427 🚇 U-Bahn Rotkreuzplatz

EILLES
www.eilles-tee.de
This small, fragrant store specializes in fine teas, coffees, chocolates, biscuits and wine. Stop here for gourmet gifts.
⊞ E5 ⊠ Donnersberger-strasse 5 ☎ 16 15 35 🚇 U-Bahn Rotkreuzplatz

ESPRESSO & BARISTA
www.listino-prezzi.com
Espresso & Barista is an atmospheric café-cum-shop specializing in everything to do with coffee: cups, machines, drinking, even coffee courses.
⊞ E5 ⊠ Schlörstrasse 11 ☎ 1678 3878 🚇 U-Bahn Rotkreuzplatz

KARSTADT
www.karstadt.de
This friendly branch of the popular Hertie department store chain stretches from the main train station to Karlsplatz and offers everyday fashion and household items at reasonable prices.
⊞ H7 ⊠ Bahnhofplatz

HANDCRAFTED PORCELAIN

The manufacture of exquisite porcelain figurines and dishes was started in 1747 by Prince Elector Maximilian III Joseph at his Nymphenburg Palace (▷ 84–85) in suburban Munich. Today about 85 artists and artisans keep alive traditional methods at a cramped factory across from the palace, throwing, forming and painting each piece by hand. Their delicate creations range from bowls and cups to graceful dancers and animals.

☎ 5 51 20 🚇 U- or S-Bahn Hauptbahnhof

KRISTINA SACK
www.kristina-sack.de
Fantastic kitchenware shop full of stylish tableware, quirky gifts and useful kitchen utensils. A must for all chefs!
⊞ E6 ⊠ Wilderich-Lang-Strasse 6 ☎ 502 3464 🚊 Tram 16, 17

OLYMPIA EINKAUFS-ZENTRUM (OEZ)
www.olympia-einkaufszen-trum.de
If you like to find everything you could ever need under one roof, visit this huge shopping complex with over 100 shops near the Olympiapark.
⊞ E1 ⊠ Hanauer Strasse 68 ☎ 1433 2910 🚇 U-Bahn Olympia Einkaufszentrum

PORZELLAN-MANUFAKTUR NYMPHENBURG
www.nymphenburg.com
This factory once created porcelain for the royal family and it still turns out beautifully handcrafted traditional designs. There is another outlet at Odeonsplatz (▷ 56).
⊞ C4 ⊠ Nördliches Schlossrondell 8 ☎ 179 1970 🕐 Mon–Fri 10–5 🚊 Tram 17

WEIHNACHTSMARKT
A small, friendly Christmas market situated beside the Kaufhof department store at Rotkreuzplatz.
⊞ E5 ⊠ Rotkreuzplatz 🚇 U-Bahn Rotkreuzplatz

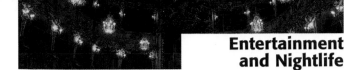

Entertainment and Nightlife

BLADE NIGHT

www.muenchnerbladenight.de
Join tens of thousands of local rollerbladers touring the city on designated Blade Nights, every Monday night from May to September. Check website for times and routes.

🔳 F6 ✉ Start in Wredestrasse (near Hackerbrücke) 🚇 S-Bahn Hackerbrücke

CAFÉ AM BEETHOVENPLATZ

www.mariandl.com
Munich's oldest "concert-café" combines the atmosphere of an old-style Viennese coffee house with a Bavarian-style beer garden.

🔳 G8 ✉ Goethestrasse 51 ☎ 552 9100 🕐 9am–1am 🚇 U-Bahn Goetheplatz 🚌 58

CAFÉ NEUHAUSEN

www.cafeneu.de
You can mingle with the in-crowd at this stylish café with its long list of long drinks.

🔳 F5 ✉ Blutenbergstrasse 106 ☎ 1897 5570 🕐 9am–1am 🚇 U-Bahn Rotkreuzplatz

CINEMA

www.cinema-muenchen.com
Probably the best cinema in town.

🔳 G6 ✉ Nymphenburgerstrasse 31 ☎ 55 52 55 🚇 U-Bahn Stiglmaierplatz

CIRCUS KRONE

www.circus-krone.de
Munich's internationally acclaimed circus offers shows from December to April.

🔳 G6 ✉ Zirkus-Krone-Strasse 1-6 ☎ 5 45 80 00 🚇 S-Bahn Hackerbrücke

MISTER B'S

www.misterbs.de
A small and very atmospheric jazz bar with nightly live jazz concerts at 10pm.

🔳 G8 ✉ Herzog-Heinrich-Strasse 38 ☎ 53 49 01 🕐 Tue–Sun 8pm–3am 🚇 U-Bahn Goetheplatz

NACHTGALERIE

www.nachtgalerie.de
This former warehouse has plenty of dance space and is a popular venue for live bands.

🔳 D7 ✉ Landsbergerstrasse 185 ☎ 3 45 55 952 🕐 Fri–Sat 10.30pm–4am 🚇 S-Bahn Donnersbergerbrücke 🚋 Tram 18, 19

OUTDOOR MUNICH

The Englischer Garten (English Garden ▷ 64–65) is a popular place for Munich's city dwellers to walk, cycle or sunbathe. This extensive green space stretches all the way from the middle of the city along the banks of the River Isar. The Olympiapark (▷ 82–83), the stadium site of the 1972 Olympic Games, has been converted into a park with facilities including swimming, tennis and ice-skating.

OLYMPIA-EISSTADION

www.olympiapark.de
Try your hand at curling or the bobsleigh push, traditional Alpine sports. Events held at the Olympic Ice Stadium.

🔳 G2 ✉ Olympiapark ☎ 30 67-0 🚇 U-Bahn Olympiazentrum

OLYMPIA-EIS-SPORTZENTRUM

www.olympiapark.de
Rent your ice skates at the door and enjoy this magnificent rink.

🔳 G2 ✉ Olympiapark ☎ 30 67-0 🚇 U-Bahn Olympiazentrum

RIVER TRIP

www.Isarflossfahrt.net
For one of Bavaria's most enjoyable experiences, take a *Gaudiflossenfahrt*; a pleasure raft trip on the River Isar from Wolfratshausen to Thalkirchen. You will drift downstream in a convoy to the music of a brass band and a steady flow of beer from the barrels on board.

🔳 G7 ✉ Bahnhofplatz 2 ☎ 1308 5890 🚇 U- or S-Bahn Hauptbahnhof

SUMMER FESTIVAL

www.olympiapark.de
Throughout the summer the Olympic Park hosts cinema on the giant screen by the lake, firework displays, music concerts, circus and other spectacular shows.

🔳 G2 ✉ Olympiapark ☎ 30 67-0 🚇 U-Bahn Olympiazentrum

WEST MUNICH ENTERTAINMENT AND NIGHTLIFE

Restaurants

PRICES

Prices are approximate, based on a 3-course meal for one person.

€€€	over €50
€€	€25–€50
€	under €25

AUGUSTINER-KELLER (€)

www.augustinerkeller.de
One of Munich's most traditional beer cellars, just a few minutes' walk from the main station. Its popular beer garden seats over 5,000, making it one of the city's largest, after the Hirschgarten and the Chinesischer Turm.
➕ G6 ✉ Arnulfstrasse 52 ☎ 59 43 93 🕐 11.30am–1am 🚇 S-Bahn Hackerbrücke 🚋 Tram 16, 17

CAFÉ RUFFINI (€)

www.ruffini.de
The vegetarian menu served here is outstanding and the occasional meat dishes are equally good.
➕ E4 ✉ Orffstrasse 22–24 ☎ 16 11 60 🕐 Tue–Sun 10am–midnight 🚇 U-Bahn Rotkreuzplatz

HACKER-PSCHORR BRÄUHAUS (€–€€)

www.hacker-pschorrbraeu.de
Ox-on-the-spit, the house specialty, is served to the accompaniment of traditional Bavarian music.
➕ F7 ✉ Theresienhöhe 7 ☎ 500 593800 🕐 10am–midnight 🚇 U-Bahn Theresienwiese

HIRSCHGARTEN (€)

www.hirschgarten.de
Munich's largest beer garden, seating 8,500, is near Schloss Nymphenburg. Children love the deer enclosure and huge park.
➕ C5 ✉ Hirschgarten 1 ☎ 1799 9119 🕐 Daily 9am–midnight 🚋 Tram 17

LÖWENBRÄUKELLER (€)

www.loewenbraeukeller.com
During the Lenten Strong Beer Season, men from all over Bavaria visit this beer cellar to pit their strength against each other in a stone-lifting competition.
➕ G6 ✉ Nymphenburger Strasse 2 ☎ 5472 6690 🕐 Daily 10am–midnight 🚇 U-Bahn Stiglmaierplatz 🚋 Tram 20, 21

ROMANS (€€–€€€)

www.ristorante-romans.de
Friendly restaurant with a large garden terrace.

OKTOBERFEST

The world's biggest beer festival commences on the third Saturday in September when the Lord Mayor taps open the first barrel with the welcome cry "O' zapft is" ("It's open") and the massive beer binge begins. Each year around 7 million visitors consume a staggering 6 million liters (over 1 million gallons) of beer, 90 spit-roast oxen and over 400,000 sausages.

Good choice of mains as well as pizza and pasta.
➕ G6 ✉ Augustenstrasse 7 ☎ 5454 7799 🕐 Mon–Sat 8–1am, Sun 10–6 🚇 U- or S-Bahn Hauptbahnhof 🚋 Tram 20, 21

SARCLETTI (€)

www.sarcletti.de
The largest ice-cream menu in town, with more than 100 flavors.
➕ E5 ✉ Nymphenburgerstrasse 155 ☎ 15 53 14 🚇 U-Bahn Rotkreuzplatz

SCHLOSSCAFÉ IM PALMENHAUS (€–€€)

www.palmenhaus.de
An elegant café in the Nymphenburg Palace's giant palm house.
➕ B4 ✉ Schloss Nymphenburg ☎ 17 53 09 🕐 Tue–Fri 11–6, Sat–Sun 10–6, Jan–Feb 10–5 🚋 51; tram 12, 16, 17

TAXISGARTEN (€)

www.taxisgarten.de
A quiet, shady spot near the Nymphenburg Palace renowned for spare ribs.
➕ E4 ✉ Taxisstrasse 12 ☎ 15 68 27 🕐 Daily 11.30–11pm 🚇 U-Bahn Gern

ZUR SCHWAIGE (€€)

www.schlosswirtschaft-schwaige.de
Traditional fare in the south wing of Schloss Nymphenburg (▷ 84–85), or in the garden.
➕ B4 ✉ Schloss Nymphenburg ☎ 1202 0890 🕐 Daily 11.30am–11pm 🚋 51; tram 12, 16, 17

Farther Afield

There is even more to see outside of Munich's city center. Bavaria has many attractions including several beautiful palaces, such as King Ludwig's fairy-tale castle, Neuschwanstein.

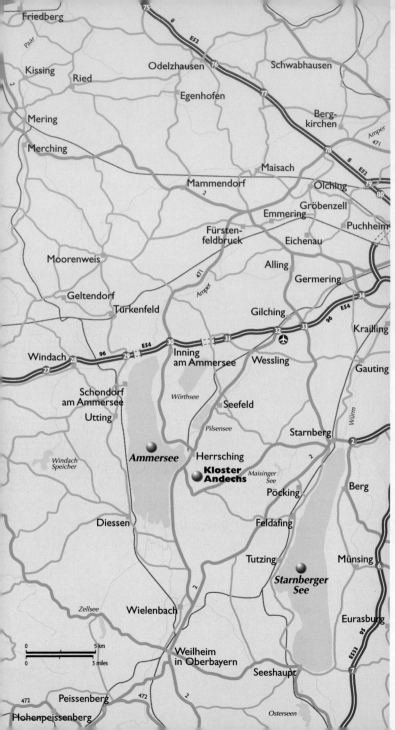

Röhrmoos

Freising

Hallbergmoos

Haimhausen

Neufahrn
bei Freising

Eching

Unter-
schleissheim

Ober-
schleissheim

Garching
bei München

Dachau

Speichersee

Schleissheim

Flugwerft
Schleissheim

Ismaning

Karlsfeld

FELD-
MOCHING

HARTHOF

Allianz
Arena

Pl4ening

FASANERIE-
NORD

Kirchheim
bei Müchen

ALLACH

Unterföhring

MENZING

MOOSACH

NYMPHEN

SCHWABING

OBER-
FÖHRING

DAGLFING

Feldkirchen

NEUAUBING

MÜNCHEN

BOGENHAUSEN

FREIHAM

PASING

LAIM

KIRCH-
TRUDERING

Vaterstetten

Gräfelfing

FÜRSTEN-
RIED

Zum
Flaucher

GIESING

BERG
AM LAIM

RAMERS-
DORF

WALD-
TRUDERING

Planegg

THAL-
KIRCHEN

Grasbrunn

Neuried

FORSTEN-
RIED
SOLLN

Tierpark
Hellabrunn

PERLACH

Neubiberg

Rutzbrunn

Bavaria
Filmstadt

Unterhaching

Ottobrunn

Pullach
im Isartal

Waldwirtschaft
Grosshesselohe

Taufkirchen

Hohenbrunn

Baierbrunn

Grünwald

Siegertsbrunn

Höhenkirchen

Oberhaching

Strasslach

Brunnthal

Schäftlarn

Dingharting

Sauerlach

Aying

Icking

Egling

Wolfratshausen

Valley

Holzkirchen

Geretsried

Dietramszell

Kirchsee

Königsdorf

Waakirchen

Isar

Bavaria Filmstadt

HIGHLIGHTS

● Stunt show
● 4-D movie experience
● Model submarine for
Das Boot

TIP

● Phone in advance to see if there is to be any TV recording during your visit, and request tickets to be part of the audience.

Glimpse behind the scenes of Europe's largest film studios, and learn the tricks of the trade. Since its renovation, Munich's "Hollywood by the Isar" has more glitz and glamor than ever before.

Film Studios Founded in 1919, the Bavaria Film Studios has hosted major Hollywood productions as well as home-grown films. In the early 1970s, *Cabaret* was filmed here, starring Liza Minelli and Michael York, and directed by Bob Fosse.

Famous films In the 1980s, the studios became famous for Wolfgang Petersen's movies, such as *Das Boot*, *Enemy Mine* and *The Never Ending Story*. It was at this time that the Bavaria Film Tours began, and today you can still visit the fascinating sets for all three films.

At the Bavaria Stunt Show at these film studios you can learn how dangerous stunts are staged, while the film workshop allows school groups to shoot their own movie

Film tours Tours of the film studios last 90 minutes (with an English-language tour at 1pm daily). Older children will love directing their own films, and even playing the starring role in a thriller under coaching from one of the studio's directors. Explore familiar film sets (including an entire Berlin street, and the Gaulish village from *Asterix and Obelix versus Caesar*), watch actors at work filming local soap opera *Marienhof*, and be sure to see the breathtaking stuntmen in action in the Bavaria Stunt Show (which takes place on the set of a deserted New York suburb) with all its special effects and daring tricks. There is a thrilling 4-D motion cinema, where your seats move with the action in the film.

Munich also boasts more than its fair share of cinemas (over 84). Some show the films in their original language.

THE BASICS

www.filmstadt.de
🚏 Off map to south
✉ Bavariafilmplatz 7
☎ 64 99 35 57
🕐 Mid-Apr to early Nov daily 9–6 (last admission 4.30pm); early Nov to mid-Mar daily 9–5pm
🚃 Tram 25
👋 Expensive
❓ Guided tours in English daily 1pm

Dachau

HIGHLIGHTS

- Schloss Dachau and Hofgarten
- Dachauer Art Gallery
- Museum
- The memorial

TIP

- For a general overview, start by watching a 22-minute documentary called "The Dachau Concentration Camp," shown at 10, 11.30, 12.30, 2 and 3pm in English, and at 9.30, 11, 1.30, 2.30 and 3.30pm in German.

Once people visited Dachau to see the Renaissance chateau and town, until it became synonymous with the Nazi reign of terror. Today the concentration camp (KZ-Gedenkstätte) has been preserved as a memorial to those who died here.

Summer castle The pretty little town of Dachau, with its 18th-century pastel facades and quaint cobbled streets, is set on the steep bank of the River Amper. The Renaissance castle above the town was once a popular summer residence of the Munich royals. Only one wing of the original four survives; it contains a large banquet hall with one of the most exquisitely carved ceilings in Bavaria. Nearby is the Dachauer Moos, a heath area often wreathed in mists, with a delicate light that is loved by artists.

Although Dachau is home to a former concentration camp, it is also a lovely historic town that deserves to be explored in its own right

FARTHER AFIELD TOP 25

The camp Munich residents used to come to Dachau to wander its picturesque streets and visit the castle. But on 22 March 1933, only 50 days after Hitler came to power, Dachau was designated as the site of the first concentration camp of the Third Reich. Although it was not one of the main extermination camps, 31,951 deaths were recorded here between 1933 and 1945. Some original buildings have been restored as a memorial, a poignant reminder of the fate of the camp's 206,000 inmates. The museum documents the camp's history and the atrocities that happened here, with the help of polyglot audio guides. There are tours in English at 1.30 (Tuesday–Friday), and 12 and 1.30 (Saturday, Sunday) in summer; and 1.30 (Thursday, Saturday, Sunday) in winter. The gates still bear the bitterly ironic slogan *"Arbeit macht frei"* ("Work makes you free").

THE BASICS

www.kz-gedenkstaette-dachau.de
✚ Off map to northwest
Ⓢ S-Bahn Dachau

Concentration Camp
✉ Alte Römerstrasse 75
☎ (08131) 752 87
🕐 Daily 9–5
🚌 S-Bahn to Dachau, then bus 726 to KZ-Gedenkstätte Haupteingang or 724 to KZ-Gedenkstätte Parkplatz
♿ Excellent
🖐 Free

Schleissheim

The Old Palace now houses collections from the Bavarian National Museum

THE BASICS

www.schloesser.bayern.de
🚩 Off map to north
☎ 315 8720
🕐 Apr–Sep Tue–Sun 9–6; Oct–Mar 10–4
🚉 S-Bahn Oberschleissheim
🚌 292
♿ None
💶 Old Palace: inexpensive; New/Lustheim: moderate; combined ticket: expensive

HIGHLIGHTS

Old Palace
● Religious folk art
New Palace
● Great Gallery
Palace Lustheim
● Meissen Porcelain
Museum

The three Schleissheim palaces capture the splendor of Munich's past. Make sure you see the Great Gallery, the delightful French-style gardens and the magnificent display of Meissen porcelain.

Old Palace In 1597 Duke Wilhelm V bought a farm to the east of the Dachau moor as a retirement residence. His son, Prince Elector Maximilian I, later transformed it into an Italian-style Renaissance palace, and called it the Altes Schloss Schleissheim. Today it contains part of the Bavarian National Museum, including an unusual gallery devoted to international religious folk art.

New Palace The beautiful Neues Schloss, the Versailles of Munich, was commissioned by Prince Elector Max Emanuel II as a summer residence. The largest palace complex of its day, it demonstrated his wealth and power. Despite severe damage during World War II, the sumptuous rococo interior remains largely intact. The Great Gallery, over 60m (197ft) long, contains the Bavarian State Art Collection. One of the most remarkable collections of baroque paintings in Europe, it includes masterpieces by Rubens, Titian, Veronese and van Dyck.

Palace Lustheim Separated from the New Palace by formal gardens and encircled by a decorative canal, Palace Lustheim was planned as an island of happiness for Max Emanuel's bride Maria Antonia. It now houses Germany's largest collection of Meissen porcelain.

More to See

ALLIANZ ARENA

www.allianz-arena.de

Munich's stadium is home to both its football (soccer) clubs—FC Bayern München and TSV 1860. Opened in 2005, it seats 69,900. Its futuristic facade, comprising nearly 3,000 inflated translucent foil panels, has earned it the nicknames "life belt" and "rubber dinghy." It changes color, red or blue, depending on which home team is playing.

➕ Off map to northeast ✉ Werner-Heisenberg-Allee 25 ☎ 6993 1222/3509
🕐 Daily 10–6 except on home match days
♿ Excellent 🚇 U-Bahn Fröttmaning
Guided tours daily in English 1pm

AMMERSEE

www.ammersee-region.de

Ammersee, with its lake promenades and sandy beaches, is set in lush green countryside at the heart of Munich's lake district, easily reached by S-Bahn. Highlights include a trip on Bavaria's oldest paddle-steamer and Kloster Andechs (▷ 102). The lake has a curious phenomenon: a

Schaukelwelle (rocking wave), which goes back and forth like a giant pendulum every 24 minutes, the water rising and falling about 10cm (4in) against the shore.

➕ Off map to southwest 🚈 S-Bahn Herrsching

FLUGWERFT SCHLEISSHEIM

www.deutsches-museum.de

A must for plane buffs, this is an extension of the Deutsches Museum's aviation display.

➕ Off map to north ✉ Effnerstrasse 18, Oberschleissheim ☎ 315 7140 🕐 Daily 9–5 🚈 S-Bahn Oberschleissheim 🚌 292
💷 Moderate

FREISING

www.freising.de

On the left bank of the River Isar, 32km (20 miles) northeast of Munich, Freising's hilltop Dom (cathedral) dates from the 12th century and has a lavish baroque interior from the 18th century.

➕ Off map to northeast 🚈 S-Bahn to Freising

The glowing "rubber dinghy" of Allianz Arena

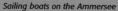

Sailing boats on the Ammersee

KLOSTER ANDECHS

www.andechs.de

One of Germany's most important pilgrimage destinations, famous for its centuries-old brewing tradition and its *Andechser Bock* beer.

✚ Off map to southwest ✉ Bergstrasse 2, Andechs ☎ 01852 3760 ◷ The various elements of the complex have different opening times ⊕ S-Bahn Herrsching then by local bus ✋ Free

STARNBERGER SEE

www.starnbergersee-info.de

The largest of the five lakes just south of the city, its banks still lined with the baroque palaces of Bavaria's aristocracy, remains the domain of the rich and famous. Today, the area offers horseback-riding, golf, swimming and sailing.

✚ Off map to southwest ⊕ S-Bahn Tutzing (and earlier lakeside stations)

TIERPARK HELLABRUNN ZOO

www.tierpark-hellabrunn.de

The whole family will enjoy a vist here, the world's first Geo-Zoo with animals grouped in habitats according to their regions of origin.

✚ Off map to south ✉ Tierparkstrasse 30 ☎ 62 50 80 ◷ Apr–Sep daily 8–6; Oct–Mar daily 9–5 ⊕ U-Bahn Thalkirchen 🚌 52 ✋ Expensive

WALDWIRTSCHAFT GROSSHESSELOHE

www.waldwirtschaft.de

A long-time local beer garden haunt overlooking the Isar gorge and famous for its live jazz.

✚ Off map to south ✉ Georg-Kalb-Strasse 3 ☎ 74 99 40 30 ◷ Daily 11–11 ⊕ S-Bahn Grosshesselohe Isartalbahnhof

ZUM FLAUCHER

www.zum-flaucher.de

Somewhat off the tourist track, this scenic beer garden is next to the River Isar. Join the local families and bring a picnic here in the evening.

✚ Off map to south ✉ Isarauen 8 ☎ 723 2677 ◷ Daily 11–11 (restaurant open Sat–Sun 11–6 only in winter) ⊕ U-Bahn Brudermühlstrasse 🚌 54

Starnberger See, with the Alps in the background

Excursions

AUGSBURG

Bavaria's oldest city has a 2,000-year history and you'll find styles of all the major architectural periods. The Renaissance flourished here, and rococo became known as the Augsburg style.

Augsburg is Bavaria's third largest city, and its oldest, founded in 15BC as the Roman legionary fortress Augusta Vindelicorum. The city has many great buildings, monumental fountains and grand boulevards, as well as 15 museums and art galleries to visit. The Renaissance Rathaus dominates Rathausplatz; inside, the restored Goldener Saal (Golden Hall) is famous for its magnificent portals, ceiling and mural paintings. The Fuggerei (1514–23) are the oldest almshouses in the world. On Frauentorstrasse is Mozart House, the birthplace of Leopold Mozart, father of Wolfgang Amadeus, and now a Mozart museum.

THE BASICS

www.augsburg-tourismus.de
Distance: 72km (45miles)
Journey Time: 30–40 mins by train
🚉 Augsburg
ℹ️ Rathausplatz 1, 86150 Augsburg
☎ 0821 502 0721

BAD TÖLZ

The beautiful spa town of Bad Tölz, at the foot of the Bavarian Alps, is famous for its iodine-rich springs and peat baths.

The elegant cobbled main street, lined with handsome pastel-colored houses ornately decorated with murals, leads up to the twin-spired Kreuzkirche noted for its Leonhard chapel. Bad Tölz is a perfect base for skiing and other mountain activities. Nearby Blombergbahn is Germany's longest summer toboggan run and the scene in winter of a crazy sled-flying competition.

THE BASICS

www.badtoelz.de
Distance: 40km (25 miles)
Journey Time: 1 hour by train
🚉 Hourly trains from the main station
ℹ️ Max-Höfler-Platz 1, 83646 Bad Tölz
☎ 08041 78670

CHIEMSEE

Locally called the Bavarian Sea, Chiemsee is the largest of the Bavarian lakes. Its lush scenery and picture-postcard Alpine backdrop has attracted artists for centuries and today draws visitors to its shores for swimming, sailing and other pursuits.

The lake's main attraction is Herrenchiemsee, site of Ludwig II's ambitious summer palace—a replica of the French Palace of Versailles. Only the central wing of the building was completed, including the spectacular Hall of Mirrors. The smaller island of Frauenchiemsee has a fishing village and a Benedictine nunnery founded in 872, where the nuns still make a special liqueur, called *Klosterlikör,* from an ancient recipe.

THE BASICS

www.chiemsee-alpenland.de
www.herren-chiemsee.de
ferry: www.chiemsee-schiffahrt.de
Distance: 80km (50 miles)
Journey Time: 1 hour by train then 30 min walk to ferry
🚆 Frequent trains to Prien from the main station
ℹ️ Chiemsee-Infocenter, Felden 10, 83233 Bernau am Chiemsee
☎ 08051 96 55 50 and (08051) 6090 (ferry)
🕐 Guided palace tours 9–5 (summer), 9.40–3.30 (winter)

SCHLOSS LINDERHOF

Set among magnificent mountain scenery and surrounded by forest, Ludwig II's Schloss Linderhof began as a hunting lodge belonging to his father, Maximilian II, and was based on the Petit Trianon at Versailles.

Completed in 1878, the lavish interiors, all decorated in Renaissance and baroque styles, include a hall of mirrors and an enormous chandelier weighing 500kg (1,000lb). Ludwig used the palace as a retreat and rarely received visitors here. The formal French gardens, fanciful fountains, grotto, Moorish kiosk and follies are a wonderful place to explore. The highlight—an exotic Moorish kiosk with a peacock throne—was acquired by Ludwig from the World Exhibition in Paris in 1876.

THE BASICS

www.linderhof.de
Distance: 100 km (62 miles)
Journey Time: 2.25 hours
🚆 Train to Oberammergau, then bus 9622
✉️ Linderhof 12, 82488 Ettal
☎ 08822 920340/421
🕐 Guided palace tours Apr–Sep daily 9–6; Oct–Mar 10–4
🖐️ Moderate

 EXCURSIONS

FARTHER AFIELD

 **THE BASICS**

www.neuschwanstein.de
Distance: 120km
(75 miles)
Journey Time: About 2
hours by train then bus 73
to Hohenschwangau and
walk uphill
🚉 Füssen
☎ 08362 930830
🕐 Guided tours Apr–Sep
daily 9–6; Oct–Mar 10–3
🚌 Daily excursions with
Visitor Tours
ℹ️ Tourist Information
Schwangau, Münchener
Strasse 2, 87645 Schwangau

 **SCHLOSS NEUSCHWANSTEIN**

This fairy-tale castle is a magical white-turreted affair nestled in a pine forest in the foothills of the Bavarian Alps. In an attempt to make the fantasy world of Wagnerian opera a reality, "Mad" King Ludwig commissioned a stage designer rather than an architect to design this romantic, theatrical castle, and watched it being built by telescope from his father's neighboring castle of Hohenschwangau.

Neuschwanstein is the most photographed building in Germany, and the inspiration for Walt Disney's Sleeping Beauty Castle at Disneyland. Sadly only 15 of the 65 rooms were finished and Ludwig spent just a few days here before he was dethroned. The lavish interior is worth lining up for, with its extravagant decor and vast wall paintings of Wagnerian scenes. Since childhood, Ludwig had a passion for German legend as epitomized in the operas of Richard Wagner. Following a performance of *Lohengrin,* Ludwig became an enthusiastic admirer and patron of Wagner, whose works inspired his eccentric building plans.

Together with Herrenchiemsee (▷ 105) and Linderhof (▷ 105), King Ludwig II's extravagant fairy-tale castles were a drain on the regency's treasury. As state affairs became increasingly neglected, the doomed monarch was declared insane and, shortly after, met a mysterious watery death on the eastern shore of the Starnberger See (▷ 102).

Fortunately, Ludwig's request to destroy Neuschwanstein on his death was ignored. Just seven weeks after his death, the castle was opened to the public to pay off the enormous debts he had incurred building it. Today, the castle is the most popular and profitable tourist attraction in Bavaria.

Munich has its quota of luxury hotels, but it also offers authentic Bavarian accommodation, and some excellent youth hostels and camping options for those on a tight budget.

Where to Stay

Introduction

There are more than 40,000 hotel beds in Munich. Budget accommodation is relatively easy to find; double rooms are better value than singles. If you are visiting in low season (November to March) you will probably be spoiled for choice—unless a large trade fair is taking place. The *Oktoberfest* (late September to early October) is a busy time, so you will need to reserve somewhere as much as a year in advance. The best advice is to always reserve ahead.

Types of Hotels

Munich has its share of well-known hotel chains, but there are still many that are family-owned. Smaller, privately owned hotels sometimes do not have any rooms designated as non-smoking, so check when you book. Air-conditioning is not standard in Munich hotels, particularly those in historic buildings, and a few may not have an elevator. A large breakfast buffet is normally included in the price in mid-range hotels. Some smaller hotels and pensions do not accept credit cards. The Upper Bavarian countryside south of Munich is also geared to welcoming tourists, so you may consider staying there and commuting by S-Bahn, train or bus.

Star Ratings

Most hotels in Germany are assigned a star rating from one to five, and prices usually reflect this. However, bear in mind that higher prices are not necessarily a guarantee of quality. For this reason, it's always a good idea to ask to see a room before booking, or if you're making a reservation online, look at any pictures.

JUGENDHERBERGEN

The Germans are mad about hostels ("Jugendherbergen") and hosteling. Facilities are generally good, but some hostels require visitors to vacate the building during the day, and others have a curfew (although this is usually sensibly late). For reservations and further information, visit www.djh-ris.de, which has an English version.

Budget Hotels

PRICES

Expect to pay up to €100 per night for a budget hotel.

A&O

www.aohostels.com
Low-price backpacker's hotel near the station and a popular budget base for the Oktoberfest.
H7 ✉ Bayerstrasse 75 ☎ 4523 5700 🚇 U- or S-Bahn Hauptbahnhof

ACANTHUS

www.acanthushotel.de
A generous breakfast served until late, along with a phone, minibar and TV in the 36 rooms.
H8 ✉ An der Hauptfeuerwache 14 ☎ 231880 🚇 Sendlinger Tor

BELLE BLUE

www.hotel-belleblue.de
This modern, minimalist pension is located near the main railway station and has 30 rooms.
G7 ✉ Schillerstrasse 21 ☎ 550 6260 🚇 U- or S-Bahn Hauptbahnhof

BLAUER BOCK

www.hotelblauerbock.de
A central hotel with 75 rooms and parking facilities. Great value.
J7 ✉ Sebastiansplatz 9 ☎ 23 17 80 🚇 U- or S-Bahn Marienplatz

BURG SCHWANECK

www.burgschwaneck.de
Excellent value, if a long way out of the city, in a castle overlooking the River Isar. Youth hostel pass required.
➕ Off map to south ✉ Burgweg 10, Pullach ☎ 7448 6670 🚇 S-Bahn Pullach

DAS HOTEL IN MÜNCHEN

www.das-hotel-in-muenchen.de
A clean, friendly pension with 32 rooms in the popular university district a short distance from the three Pinakothek galleries.
J5 ✉ Türkenstrasse 35 ☎ 2 88 14 00 🚇 U-Bahn Universität

GÄSTEHAUS ENGLISCHER GARTEN

www.hotelenglischergarten.de
An oasis on the edge of the English Garden; only 12 rooms in the main building and 13 in the annex. Reserve well ahead.
K4 ✉ Liebergesellstrasse 8 ☎ 383 9410 🚇 U-Bahn Münchner Freiheit

CAMPING

For really cheap accommodation in Munich, why not bring a tent? There are many campsites in and around Munich. The best, and the most central, is Camping Thalkirchen (☎ 723 1707; www.muenchen.de) attractively positioned along the River Isar, with 700 places open from mid-March until the end of October. There is no need to reserve except during the Oktoberfest.

HAUS INTERNATIONAL

www.haus-international.de
Slightly more expensive than youth hostels, but you don't have to belong to a youth hostel organization to stay here.
H4 ✉ Elisabethstrasse 87 ☎ 12 00 60 🚇 U-Bahn Hohenzollernplatz

JUGENDHERBERGE MÜNCHEN (MUNICH CITY YOUTH HOSTEL)

www.jugendherberge.de
Advance reservations and a youth hostel pass are essential here.
E5 ✉ Wendl-Dietrich-Strasse 20 ☎ 2024 4490 🚇 U-Bahn Rotkreuzplatz

MITWOHNBÖRSE– HOME COMPANY

www.muenchen.home company.de
Useful for longer stays, the Mitwohnzentrale will arrange self-catering apartment accommodation in Munich for a small fee.
K3 ✉ Germaniastrasse 20 ☎ 1 94 45 🚇 U-Bahn Dietlindenstrasse

SMART STAY HOSTEL

www.munichcity.smart-stay.de
The clean and brightly furnished rooms at this invariably bustling modern hostel range from singles and doubles to 4, 6 and 8-bed units. All are handily placed for the Oktoberfest.
G8 ✉ Mozartstrasse 4 ☎ 55 87970 🚇 U-Bahn Goetheplatz

WHERE TO STAY BUDGET HOTELS

109

Mid-Range Hotels

WHERE TO STAY MID-RANGE HOTELS

ADMIRAL
www.hotel-admiral.de
This smart hotel with 33
rooms, near the river,
offers special weekend
packages.
➕ J8 ✉ Kohlstrasse 9
☎ 21 63 50 🚇 S-Bahn
Isartor

AM MARKT
www.hotel-am-markt.eu
A traditional hotel with
31 rooms, on one
of the last original
old squares near the
Viktualienmarkt.
➕ J7 ✉ Heiliggeiststrasse 6
☎ 22 50 14 🚇 U- or S-Bahn
Marienplatz

ANNA
www.annahotel.de
A tasteful, modern hotel
with 56 rooms, near to
the main railway station,
with underground parking
facilities and young,
helpful staff.
➕ H7 ✉ Schützenstrasse 1
☎ 59 99 40 🚇 U- or S-Bahn
Hauptbahnhof

ANTARES
www.antares-muenchen.de
Offering simple, afford-
able accommodation
in the heart of the city,
this friendly hotel is ideally located near the
popular Leopoldstrasse
shopping thoroughfare,
and the Pinakothek art
galleries.
➕ J6 ✉ Amalienstrasse 20
☎ 28 00 200 🚇 U-Bahn
Odeonsplatz

CARLTON
www.carlton-astoria.de
A hidden treasure for
those in the know, this
49-room hotel, close to
Odeonsplatz, is reason-
ably priced.
➕ J6 ✉ Fürstenstrasse 12
☎ 38 39 630 🚇 U-Bahn
Odeonsplatz

CORTIINA
www.cortiina.com
Smart, minimalist hotel
frequented by a super-
chic clientele. Internet
portal in all 35 rooms.
➕ J7 ✉ Ledererstrasse 8
☎ 242 2490 🚇 U- or
S-Bahn Marienplatz

COSMOPOLITAN
www.cosmopolitanhotel.de
Simple, modern
hotel with 71 rooms.
Surprisingly quiet consid-
ering it is in the heart of
Schwabing.
➕ J4 ✉ Hohenzollernstrasse

5 ☎ 3 83 810 🚇 U-Bahn
Giselastrasse, Münchner
Freiheit

EXQUISIT
www.hotel-exquisit.com
A small, elegant hotel
with a choice of 50
rooms, in a secluded
side street near the
site where the
Oktoberfest takes place.
➕ H7 ✉ Pettenkoferstrasse
3 ☎ 551 990 🚇 U-Bahn
Sendlinger Tor

FLEMING'S CITY
www.flemings-hotels.com
This smart central 4-star
hotel prides itself on
its modern yet intimate
atmosphere. Facilities
include 99 stylish
rooms, all with WLAN
connections, a popular
brasserie-cum-wine bar,
and a small fitness area.
➕ H7 ✉ Bayerstrasse 47
☎ 4444 660 🚇 S-Bahn
Karlsplatz (Stachus)

FLEMING'S SCHWABING
www.flemings-hotels.com
In the Schwabing area,
this modern, 168-room
hotel makes a good base
for sightseeing and dining
out. It boasts a brasserie,
wine bar, delicatessen
and, in summer months,
a beer terrace.
➕ K3 ✉ Leopoldstrasse
130–132 ☎ 206 0900
🚇 U-Bahn Dietlindenstrasse

GÄSTEHAUS ENG-LISCHER GARTEN
www.hotelenglischergarten.de
An oasis on the edge

of the English Garden. Twelve rooms in the main building, 13 in the annex. Reserve well ahead.

➕ K4 ✉ Liebergesellstrasse 8 ☎ 383 9410 🚇 U-Bahn Münchner Freiheit

HOTEL METROPOL

www.hotelmetropol.de
Rooms in this newly refurbished three-star hotel are comfortable and quiet, considering the hotel is so close to the Hauptbahnhof. About 25 rooms have a balcony.

➕ G7 ✉ Millererstrasse 7 ☎ 2444 9990 🚇 U- or S-Bahn Hauptbahnhof

INSEL MÜHLE

www.inselmuehle-muenchen.com
This beautifully renovated, timbered corn mill is one of the Romantik chain of hotels and has 37 rooms. Just outside the city but worth the extra trip.

➕ Off map to west ✉ Von-Kahr-Strasse 87 ☎ 8 10 10 🚇 S-Bahn Allach

MARIANDL

www.hotelmariandl.de
A gem of a hotel just southwest of the city center, the Mariandl has gracefully furnished rooms set in a turreted town house, and with the Café am Beethovenplatz (▷ 91) on the ground floor.

➕ G8 ✉ Goethestrasse 51 ☎ 552 9100 🚇 U-Bahn Goetheplatz 🚋 58

PENSION SEIBEL

www.seibel-hotels-munich.de
This pension has bags of charm with traditional Bavarian decoration in the rooms and breakfast room. The location is great too—just behind the Viktualienmarkt (▷ 33). Book early for lower rates or stay in low season.

➕ J8 ✉ Reichenbachstrasse 8 ☎ 2319 180 🚋 Tram 17, 18

SCHLICKER

www.hotel-schlicker.de
Good value hotel in a central location, near Marienplatz. The rooms overlooking busy Tal are double-glazed. Choose from doubles, triples, suites and a split-level maisonette.

➕ J7 ✉ Tal 8 ☎ 242 8870 🚇 U- or S-Bahn Marienplatz

SEIBEL'S PARK

www.seibel-hotels-munich.de
This hotel is owned by the same family as Pension Seibel (▷ this page), but is not as

central. Rooms are large with a radio, cable TV and telephone. There is also a sauna, to relax in after a hard day's sightseeing.

➕ Off map to west ✉ Maria-Eich-Strasse 32 ☎ 829 9520 🚇 S-Bahn Pasing

SPLENDID-DOLLMANN

www.hotel-splendid-dollmann.de
A small, exclusive hotel in central Munich, with 37 rooms decorated in a range of styles including baroque, Louis XIV and Bavarian.

➕ K7 ✉ Thierschstrasse 49 ☎ 23 80 80 🚇 U-Bahn Lehel

ST. PAUL

www.hotel-stpaul.de
Ideally situated for the Oktoberfest ground, St. Paul has rooms with a safe, television, telephone and internet access. You can eat outside in the little courtyard in summer.

➕ G7 ✉ St-Paul-Strasse 7 ☎ 5440 7800 🚇 U-Bahn Theresienwiese

TORBRÄU

www.torbraeu.de
This friendly, central hotel is the oldest in Munich, founded in 1490, and run by the same family for nearly 100 years. Its 91 rooms cater to families, individuals and business visitors. The Italian restaurant offers room service in the evenings.

➕ J7 ✉ Tal 41 ☎ 24 23 40 🚇 S-Bahn Isator

Luxury Hotels

PRICES

Expect to pay over €200 per night for a luxury hotel.

BAYERISCHER HOF
www.bayerischerhof.de
Classic, family-run hotel with excellent facilities including a roof-garden, health club, swimming pool and several top restaurants. 373 rooms.
➕ H7 ✉ Promenadeplatz 2–6 ☎ 2 12 00 🚇 U- or S-Bahn Marienplatz

EXCELSIOR
www.excelsior-hotel.de
In the tranquil pedestrian zone, three minutes' walk from the main station.
➕ H7 ✉ Schützenstrasse 11 ☎ 55 13 70 🚇 U- or S-Bahn Hauptbahnhof

HILTON PARK
www.hilton.de
The Hilton has 479 rooms plus outdoor dining, beer garden, indoor pool, business area and views over the Englischer Garten.
➕ K6 ✉ Am Tucherpark 7 ☎ 38 450 🚌 54, 154; tram 17

KEMPINSKI HOTEL VIER JAHRESZEITEN
www.kempinski-vierjahreszeiten.com
Munich's flagship hotel, placed on the city's most exclusive shopping street, and within easy walking distance of most of the city's sights. 303 rooms.
➕ J7 ✉ Maximilianstrasse 17 ☎ 21 250 🚇 U-Bahn Odeonsplatz 🚋 Tram 19

KÖNIGSHOF
www.koenigshof-hotel.de
One of Munich's top hotels with 87 rooms and one of the best restaurants in town.
➕ H7 ✉ Karlsplatz 25 ☎ 55 13 60 🚇 U- or S-Bahn Karlsplatz

MANDARIN ORIENTAL
www.mandarinoriental.com
Guests at this 73-room, luxury hotel have included Prince Charles and Madonna.
➕ J7 ✉ Neuturmstrasse 1 ☎ 29 09 80 🚇 U- or S-Bahn Marienplatz

LE MERIDIEN
www.starwoodhotels.com
This chic, new hotel opposite the main station combines old-world charm with state-of-the-art amenities in its 381 sophisticated rooms and suites, together with a soothing spa to re-invigorate visitors.
➕ H7 ✉ Bayerstrasse 41 ☎ 24 22 0 🚇 U- or S-Bahn Hauptbahnhof

OPERA
www.hotel-opera.de
A small, plush hotel, with 25 rooms, set in a delightful old mansion with an inner courtyard.
➕ K7 ✉ St-Anna-Strasse 10 ☎ 210 4940 🚇 U-Bahn Lehel

PLATZL
www.platzl.de
A friendly hotel with 167 traditional rooms. Top-class facilities include a fitness area and a beautiful restaurant in a converted mill.
➕ J7 ✉ Sparkassenstrasse 10 ☎ 23 70 30 🚇 U- or S-Bahn Marienplatz

PRINZREGENT AM FRIEDENSENGEL
www.prinzregent.de
Tradition and comfort combine at this elegant hotel, with 65 rooms and an attractive garden.
➕ L7 ✉ Ismaninger Strasse 42–44 ☎ 41 60 50 🚇 U-Bahn Max-Weber-Platz

RITZI
www.hotelritzi.de
The aptly named Ritzi is central yet quiet, with 25 stylish rooms. It has a trendy bar and serves a great buffet breakfast.
➕ L6 ✉ Maria-Theresia Strasse 2a ☎ 4142 40890 🚇 U-Bahn Max-Weber-Platz

CRÈME DE LA CRÈME

The elegant, traditional Vier Jahreszeiten (Four Seasons) hotel was established in the mid-19th century as a guesthouse for royalty visiting King Maximilian II and is still used today to accommodate visiting dignitaries. Its Vue Maximilian restaurant is well known for its superb cuisine (especially its Sunday brunch) and English afternoon tea is served in the lobby (▷ 58).

Need to Know

Everything you need to know to make your visit to Munich a success, from the initial planning stages through to practical tips on the ground to make your trip a memorable one.

Planning Ahead

When to Go

Munich is busiest between April and September when the weather is at its best. May is the start of the beer garden season while, in summer, the city is popular for its opera festival and lively park life. Autumn draws beer-lovers to the *Oktoberfest* (▷ 92) and December is crowded with shoppers who come for the Christmas market.

> **TIME**
>
> Munich is one hour ahead of the UK, six hours ahead of New York and nine hours ahead of Los Angeles.

AVERAGE DAILY MAXIMUM TEMPERATURES

JAN	FEB	MAR	APR	MAY	JUN	JUL	AUG	SEP	OCT	NOV	DEC
34°F	34°F	46°F	57°F	64°F	69°F	76°F	74°F	75°F	67°F	57°F	38°F
1°C	1°C	8°C	14°C	18°C	21°C	24°C	23°C	24°C	19°C	14°C	3°C

Spring (March to May) is at its most delightful in May, with mild days and the least rainfall.

Summer (June to August) is the sunniest season, with blue skies and long, hazy days, but also the occasional thunderstorm.

Autumn (September to November) is often still warm and sunny—the so-called *Altweibersommer* ("old wives summer").

Winter (December to February) is the coldest time of year, with frequent snowfalls.

WHAT'S ON

February *Fasching:* High-point of the carnival season, which begins in Nov.

March *Starkbierzeit:* Strong beer season.

April *Spring Festival:* A two-week mini *Oktoberfest* at the Theresienwiese.
Ballet Festival Week.
Auer Mai Dult: First of three annual fairs and flea markets.

May *May Day* (1 May): Traditional maypole dancing at the Viktualienmarkt.
Maibockzeit: A season of special strong lagers originating from North Germany.
Corpus Christi (second Thu after Whitsun): A magnificent Catholic procession dating back to 1343.

June *Spargelzeit:* Celebrates the many ways there are to serve asparagus.
Founding of Munich (14 Jun): From Marienplatz to Odeonsplatz the streets fill with music, street performances and refreshment stalls.
Film Festival: A week of international cinematic art.
Tollwood Festival: The Olympiapark hosts an alternative festival of rock, jazz, cabaret, food and folklore.

July *Opera Festival:* The climax of the cultural year.
Auer Jacobi Dult: The second annual Dult.
Kocherlball: A traditional workers' ball at 6am in the Englischer Garten.

August *Summer Festival:* Two weeks of fireworks and festivities in Olympiapark.

September *Oktoberfest:* The world's largest beer festival.

October *Auer Kirchweih Dult:* The third annual Dult.
German Art and Antiques Fair.

December *Christkindlmarkt:* Christmas market.

Munich Online

www.muenchen.de
This is the official Munich Tourist Office website, including online hotel reservations and general information on the local weather, city sights, guided tours, shopping, restaurants, nightlife and special events.

www.munichfound.de
The monthly English-language magazine *Munich Found* caters to visitors and residents alike with tips on local events, a comprehensive city guide and restaurant and nightlife listings, as well as children's sports and activities.

www.munich-partyearth.com
Up-to-date information on Munich's nightlife scene with details of all the latest concerts, bars and clubs. A must for party animals.

www.schloesser.bayern.de
A comprehensive and informative guide to the palaces, castles, fortresses, residences, parks, gardens and lakes in Munich and throughout Bavaria.

www.museen-in-bayern.de
Detailed site covering 50 museums in Munich alone, as well as in the surrounding region.

www.travelforkids.com/Funtodo/Germany/ munich.htm
Brief descriptions of attractions for children and families in and around Munich.

www.mvv-muenchen.de/en
Everything you could wish to know about the Munich transport system, with maps, electronic timetables, tickets and prices for the city's S-Bahn (urban rail), U-Bahn (underground), trams and buses.

www.biergarten.com
A comprehensive guide (in German only) to the best of Munich's beer gardens.

USEFUL TRAVEL SITES

www.munich-airport.de
For details of flight arrivals and departures, general travel information, airport facilities and transport links with the city.

www.fodors.com
A complete travel planning site. You can research prices and weather; book air tickets, cars and rooms; pose questions to fellow travelers and find links to other useful sites.

INTERNET CAFÉS

Coffee Fellows
www.coffee-fellows.de
✉ Leopoldstrasse 70 ☎ 38 89 84 70 ◷ 7am–midnight
📶 22.50 per hour

Surf Inn
www.surf-inn.net
✉ Pötschnerstrasse 5
☎ 1307 7170 ◷ Mon–Thu 9.30–8, Fri–Sat 9–8
📶 €1.50 for 30 mins

M-Fi
M-Fi is a free wireless Internet service offered by the city of Munich. The Internet can be accessed from devices in many of the cafés, restaurants and hotels, but also in the following public areas: Marienplatz, Sendlinger Tor, Odeonsplatz and Stachus. Further locations are being planned.

Getting There

ENTRY REQUIREMENTS

For the latest passport and visa information, check your relevant embassy website (UK: www.gov.uk; USA: www.usembassy.gov).

TOURIST OFFICES

www.munich-tourist.de
● **Hauptbahnhof**
✉ Bahnhofplatz 2
☎ 2339 6500
🕐 Mon–Sat 9–8, Sun 10–6;
● **Head Office (administration only)**
Tourismusamt München
✉ Sendlinger Strasse 1, 80331 München
🕐 Mon–Fri 10–8, Sat 10–4

● **Neues Rathaus**
✉ Marienplatz 8
🕐 Mon–Fri 10–8, Sat 10–4

German National Tourist Offices
www.germany.travel
● **UK** ✉ 60 Buckingham Palace Rd, London SW1W 0AH ☎ 020 7317 0914
● **US** ✉ 122 East 42nd Street, Suite 2000, New York, NY 10168–0072
☎ (212) 661 7200
● **Australia** ✉ Gate 7, 32 Crown St, Woolloomooloo NSW 2001 ☎ 02 9356 2945
● **Canada** ✉ 2 Bloor Street West, Suite 2601, Toronto, Ontario M4W 3E2
☎ (416) 935 1896

AIRPORTS

Munich's international airport, Flughafen München Franz-Josef-Strauss, is located 28km (17.5 miles) north of the city, and offers services to over 150 destinations worldwide. Facilities include a bank, pharmacy and a medical facility, as well as a variety of shops, restaurants and cafés.

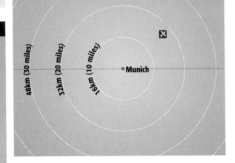

ARRIVING AT FLUGHAFEN MÜNCHEN FRANZ-JOSEF-STRAUSS

For 24-hour flight information ☎ 97 52 13 13; www.munich-airport.de

The S-Bahn (urban train network) offers two services to the city from platforms located beneath the airport's main shopping area.

S-Bahn 8 runs every 20 minutes from 4am until 1.02am, while S-Bahn 1 runs every 20 minutes from 5.50am until 12.10am, and also Monday to Friday at 4.30am and weekends at 5.30am. Buy tickets from the machines in the shopping area before going down to the platform. Remember to stamp your ticket in the blue punch-machine *(Entwerter)* on the platform to validate it before boarding the train. A single journey to the heart of the city costs €11.00. Alternatively, an airport bus leaves Munich North Terminal every 20 minutes from 6.20am to 9.40pm, taking 45 minutes to reach the main railway station. A single ticket costs €10.50.

ARRIVING BY BUS

There are frequent coach links with other German cities, starting from the main bus terminal beside the main railway station.

ARRIVING BY TRAIN

Trains take around 18 hours to Munich from Calais, in France, or Ostend, in Belgium. Munich has good connections with most major European cities. Most trains terminate at the main station (Hauptbahnhof). The east station (Ostbahnhof) takes regular motorail services from other German stations and from Paris, Budapest, Athens, Istanbul and Rimini. Train information from German Railways (Deutsche Bahn) is available in the main station's Travel Centre *(Reisezentrum)* ☎ 1308 1055.

ARRIVING BY CAR

Munich is well served by motorways (highways) and a ring road provides easy access to the city. Follow the clearly marked speed restrictions. Fines are harsh. Street parking is difficult in the heart of the city. Car parks charge around €18 a day. Try the Mühoga Münchner Hochgaragen (Adolf-Kolping-Strasse 10) or the Tiefgarage von der Opera (Max-Joseph-Platz 4).
● Car rental: Avis, www.avis.de ☎ (01805) Airport: 9759 7600, Hauptbahnhof: 550 2251

CONSULATES

● UK ✉ Möhlstrasse 5 ☎ 21 10 90
● US ✉ Königinstrasse 5 ☎ 28 880
● Canada ✉ Tal 29 ☎ 2 19 95 70

INSURANCE

Check your policy and buy any necessary supplements. EU nationals receive free emergency medical treatment with the relevant documentation (a European Health Insurance Card, EHIC) but full travel insurance is still advised and is vital for all other visitors.

CUSTOMS REGULATIONS

Duty-free limits for non-European Union visitors are: 200 cigarettes or 250g of tobacco or 50 cigars; 2 liters of wine and 1 liter of spirits.

Getting Around

DISCOUNTS

● Children under six travel free and aged six to 14 at reduced fares.

● The City Tourcard, available from tourist offices, the main train station and some hotels. Unlimited travel for 24 hours on all public transport plus savings of up to 50 percent on admission to major city attractions including museums, city tours, bicycle rentals and the zoo. The price ranges from €10.90 for a one-day card for one person, to €69.90 for a four-day family card.

VISITORS WITH DISABILITIES

Access for visitors with disabilities is generally good in Munich, although some older attractions and churches have few facilities. The Tourist Office's brochure *Munich for Physically Challenged Tourists* (in German) contains useful information on travel, lodgings, restaurants, arts and culture, city tours and leisure, and the MVV publishes a map detailing transport facilities.

For more information contact the Städtischer Beraterkreis Behinderte Geschäftsstelle (central advice bureau for people with disabilities) www. bb-m.info ✉ Burgstrasse 4 ☎ 2332 4452.

GETTING AROUND

U-Bahn (underground) and S-Bahn (suburban trains) provide a regular service within 40km (25 miles) of central Munich. Routes are referred to by their final stop. Underground trains run every 5 or 10 minutes from about 5am to 1am (later at weekends). Tickets are available from automatic ticket machines at stations, MVV sales points in many stations, or in newspaper shops. Before boarding a train, you must put your ticket in the blue punching machine *(Entwerter)*.

On buses and trams you must stamp your ticket upon boarding. Single tickets can be bought from the driver (with small change only). Multiple tickets, also valid for U- and S-Bahn, can be bought from vending machines at train stations, but not from the driver. Some trams have ticket vending machines on board. Bus and tram routes are numbered and the vehicle has a destination board showing where it is going. Two late-night bus lines Mon–Fri and six lines (Sat–Sun) and four tram lines operate between the heart of the city and the suburbs once an hour from 1.30am to 4.30am.

● Munich has an excellent, albeit complicated, public transport network, with two urban railways (S-Bahn rapid transit and U-Bahn subway), and a comprehensive network of bus and tram routes.
● The local transport authority is the Münchner Verkehrs- und Tarifverbund (MVV) ✉ Thierschstrasse 2   ☎ 4142 4344

TYPES OF TICKET
● The MVV network is divided into fare zones. Prices are based on the number of zones required to complete the trip. For most sightseeing you will remain in the *Innenraum* (interior area—marked blue on station maps). To travel farther you need a ticket valid for the *Gesamtnetz* (total network).
● Traveling without a valid ticket can result in a heavy fine.

- *Kurzstrecke*: short trip single tickets can be bought for journeys covering only four stops; two may be U- or S-Bahn stops. A trip must not last more than one hour and can only be used in one direction. Unlimited transfers are permitted.
- *Streifenkarte*: a strip of tickets. For each journey, stamp the appropriate number of strips. A short trip is one strip. More than two U- or S-Bahn stops within one zone is two strips. If you are traveling outside the blue *Innenraum* zone, a notice shows how many strips you need to punch.
- *Einzelfahrkarte*: single tickets can be bought covering any number of zones, but a Streifenkarte usually works out cheaper.
- *Tageskarte*: one day's unlimited travel from 9am until 6am the following day. Purchase either a *Single-Tageskarte* for one person, or a *Partner-Tageskarte* for up to five people (maximum two adults).
- *Isarcard*: a weekly or monthly ticket providing unlimited travel on MVV transport, available at MVV ticket offices or ticket vending machines.

THE U- AND S-BAHN
- Smoking is banned on trains and in the stations.
- Bicycles may be taken on the trains all day Sat, Sun and public holidays; on weekdays not at rush hour (6–9am, 4–6pm).

TRAMS
- Scenic routes: trams 16, 17, 18, 19, 20, 21 and 27 operate around the old town; tram 20 goes to the Englischer Garten; tram 27 is useful for exploring Schwabing.

MAPS AND TIMETABLES
- MVV station ticket offices and tourist information offices supply free maps and information.

TAXIS
- Taxis are cream-colored; stands are throughout the city. They are not particularly cheap.

WOMEN TRAVELERS
- Frauenhaus München offers 24-hour help for women, www.frauenhilfe-muenchen.de ☎ 35 48 30
- Munich airport and other city car parks have well-lit, reserved parking for women only near the main entrance. For a sauna and workout, visit My Sportlady Fitness Studio, www.my-sportlady.de ✉ Klenzestrasse 57c ☎ 201428 ⏰ Mon, Wed, Fri 8–10, Tue–Thu 7–10, Sat–Sun 9–8

STUDENT TRAVELERS
- Some museums and theaters offer up to 50 percent discounts with an International Student ID Card.
- A German Rail Youth Pass is available for young people under 26, valid for 3 to 10 days, www.germanrailpasses.com
- For budget accommodation, camping and youth hostels (▷ 109).

Essential Facts

NEED TO KNOW ESSENTIAL FACTS

TOILETS

Toiletten are marked *Herren* (men) and *Damen* (women). *Besetzt* means occupied, *frei* means vacant. There is often a small charge.

MONEY

The euro is the official currency of Germany. Bank notes are in denominations of 5, 10, 20, 50, 100, 200 and 500 euros and coins in denominations of 1, 2, 5, 10, 20 and 50 cents and 1 and 2 euros.

ELECTRICITY

● 230 (220–240) volts; two-pin sockets. Take an adaptor with you.

ETIQUETTE

● Say *Grüss Gott* (good day) and *Auf Wiedersehen* (goodbye) when shopping, *Guten Appetit* (enjoy your meal) when eating, *Entschuldigen Sie* (excuse me) in crowds.
● Never jump lights at pedestrian crossings. Don't walk on cycle paths.
● Dress is generally informal, except for at the theater, opera or in nightclubs.
● Service is officially included in bills but tipping is customary.

MEDICAL TREATMENT

● A list of English-speaking doctors is available at the British and US consulates.
● Pack enough of any prescription medication you take regularly to last for the duration of your trip.
● Every neighborhood has a 24-hour pharmacy *(Apotheke)*. Look for the address of that night's 24-hour *Apotheke* displayed in the pharmacy windows.
● International pharmacies have staff who speak different languages. Try Bahnhof-Apotheke ✉ Bahnhofplatz 2 ☎ 59 98 90 40 or Internationale Ludwigs-Apotheke ✉ Neuhauserstrasse 11 ☎ 55 05 070

NATIONAL HOLIDAYS

● 1 January, 6 January, Good Friday, Easter Sunday, Easter Monday, 1 May, Ascension Day, Whit Sunday and Whit Monday, Corpus Christi, 15 August, 3 October, 1 November, Day of Repentance and Prayer (during 3rd/4th week in November), Christmas Day, 26 December.

NEWSPAPERS AND MAGAZINES

● Bavaria's daily paper, *Süddeutsche Zeitung*, is published in Munich.

- Munich has several local dailies including the *Münchner Abendzeitung*, *tz* and *Bild-Zeitung*.
- The online site www.toytowngermany.com has a calendar of English-language events in Munich.

OPENING HOURS

- Banks: Mon–Fri 8.30–3.45 (some open Thu to 5.30, many close for lunch).
- Shops: Mon–Sat 9–6 (9–8 in the malls and shopping centers).
- Museums and galleries: Tue–Sun 9 or 10am–5. Some close Mon and public holidays. Many are free on Sunday.

PLACES OF WORSHIP

- Roman Catholic: Frauenkirche, Peterskirche, Theatinerkirche and many others.
- Roman Catholic Services in English: Sunday at 10.30am in St John Kaulbachstrasse 33 and Sunday at 6pm in Kreuzkirche, Kreuzstrasse 2.
- Jewish: ✉ Berchman's Center and Synagogue, Sankt-Jacobs-Platz
- Islamic Center and Mosque ✉ Wallnerstrasse 1–3
- English services: International Baptist Church ✉ Holzstrasse 9; Sunday at 5pm Evangelical International Community Church ✉ Mozartstrasse 12; Sunday at 3.30

POST OFFICES

- One of the largest post offices is opposite the railway station ✉ Bahnhofplatz 1 ☎ 01802 3333 🕐 Mon–Fri 8–6.30, Sat 9–4
- Most other post offices are open Mon–Fri 8–12, 3–6.30pm, Sat 9–12.
- Post boxes are bright yellow and clearly marked "Munich" and "other places" *(Andere Orte)*.
- All letters to other countries cost €0.75. There is a single rate for letters and postcards to anywhere in the world.

EMERGENCIES

- Police ☎ 110 ● Fire ☎ 112 ● Ambulance ☎ 112
- Dental emergency service ☎ 723 3093/94
- Poisons emergency service ☎ 19240
- Rape hotline ☎ 76 37 37
- Breakdown service ☎ 01802 22 22 22

LOST PROPERTY

- **Municipal lost property office:** ✉ Oetztalerstrasse 17 🕐 Mon, Wed, Fri 7.30–12; Tue 8.30–12, 2–6; Thu 8.30–3 ☎ 2 33 960 45
- For anything lost on the urban rail, underground, tram or bus, contact MVV (☎ 4142 4344) for the transport company's number.
- For items left on Deutsche Bahn trains: **Fundbüro der Bundesbahn** ✉ Hauptbahnhof, opposite platform 26 🕐 Mon–Fri 7am–8pm, Sat, Sun, Hols 8am–7pm ☎ 09001 990599

TELEPHONES

- Munich from abroad: dial 00 49, then the area code 89, followed by the number.
- From Munich: dial 00 and country code (UK 44, Ireland 353, US and Canada 1), then the number.

Language

There is one official standard German language, Hochdeutsch (High German), which everyone in the country should be able to understand. However, the regional Bavarian dialect, with a strong local accent, is widely spoken in Munich. The words and phrases that follow are High German.

BASICS	
ja	yes
nein	no
bitte	please
danke	thank you
bitte schön	you're welcome
Guten Tag/Grüss Gott	Hello
Guten Morgen	Good morning
Guten Abend	Good evening
Gute Nacht	Good night
Auf Wiedersehen	Goodbye
entschuldigen Sie bitte	excuse me please
sprechen Sie Englisch?	do you speak English?
ich verstehe nicht	I don't understand
Wiederholen Sie das, bitte	Please repeat that
Sprechen Sie langsamer bitte	Please speak more slowly
heute	today
gestern	yesterday
morgen	tomorrow
jetzt	now
gut	good
Ich heisse...	My name is...
Wie heissen Sie?	What's your name?
Ich komme aus...	I'm from...
Wie geht es Ihnen?	How are you?
Sehr gut, danke	Fine, thank you
Wie spät ist es?	What is the time?
wo	where
wann	when
warum	why
wer	who

USEFUL WORDS	
klein/gross	small/large
kalt/warm	cold/warm
rechts/links	right/left
geradeaus	straight on
nahe/weit	near/far
geschlossen/ offen	closed/ open

OUT AND ABOUT

Wieviel kostet es?	how much does it cost?
teuer	expensive
billig	inexpensive
Wo sind die Toiletten?	Where are the toilets?
Wo ist die Bank?	Where's the bank?
der Bahnhof	station
der Flughafen	airport
das Postamt	post office
die Apotheke	chemist
die Polizei	police
das Krankenhaus	hospital
der Arzt	doctor
Hilfe	help
Haben Sie einen Stadtplan?	Do you have a city map?
Fahren Sie mich bitte zum/zur/nach...	Please take me to...
Ich möchte hier aussteigen	I'd like to get out here
Ich habe mich ver-laufen/verfahren	I am lost
Können Sie mir helfen?	Can you help me?

NUMBERS

eins	1
zwei	2
drei	3
vier	4
fünf	5
sechs	6
sieben	7
acht	8
neun	9
zehn	10
elf	11
zwölf	12
dreizehn	13
zwanzig	20
einundzwanzig	21
dreissig	30
vierzig	40
fünfzig	50
sechszig	60
siebzig	70
achtzig	80
neunzig	90
hundert	100
tausend	1000
million	million

AT THE HOTEL/RESTAURANT

die Speisekarte	menu
das Frühstück	breakfast
das Mittagessen	lunch
das Abendessen	dinner
der Weisswein	white wine
der Rotwein	red wine
das Bier	beer
das Brot	bread
die Milch	milk
der Zucker	sugar
das Wasser	water
die Rechnung	bill (check)
das Zimmer	room
Ich bin allergisch gegen	I am allergic to
Ich bin Vegetarier	I am a vegetarian

COLORS

schwarz	black
blau	blue
braun	brown
rot	red
grün	green
weiss	white
gelb	yellow
rosa	pink
orange	orange
grau	grey
lila	purple

Timeline

LUDIWG I, II AND III

Between 1825 and 1848 King Ludwig I transformed Munich into the Athens on the Isar, a flourishing hub of art and learning, and a university city.

In 1848 the king abdicated following political unrest and an affair with the dancer Lola Montez.

In 1886 Ludwig II was certified insane and later found mysteriously drowned in the Starnberger See.

King Ludwig III was deposed in 1918 in the Bavarian Revolution, led by Kurt Eisner, Bavaria's first Prime Minister.

777 First recorded mention of Munichen ("the home of the monks").

1158 Henry the Lion founds Munich.

1327 Munich suffers a devastating fire.

1328 Ludwig IV is made Holy Roman Emperor and Munich becomes temporarily the imperial capital.

1505 Munich becomes the capital of Bavaria.

1634 The plague reduces Munich's population by one third, to 9,000.

1806 Bavaria becomes a kingdom.

1810 A horse race celebrating the marriage of Crown Prince Ludwig starts the tradition of the *Oktoberfest.*

1864 Composer Richard Wagner moves to Munich.

1876 The first trams run in the city.

1900 Munich becomes a focus of the Jugendstil (art nouveau) movement.

1919 The assassination in Munich of Bavaria's first Prime Minister, Kurt Eisner, results in a communist republic.

(From left to right) Jugendstilhaus Ainmillerstrasse; Schloss Linderhof; Schloss Neuschwanstein; tapestry from Neuschwanstein; decoration from the Jugendstilhaus

1933 Hitler comes to power.

1939 World War II commences.

1940 First air attack on Munich.

1945 American troops take Munich.

1946 Munich becomes the capital of the Free State of Bavaria.

1972 A terrorist attack ends the 20th Summer Olympic Games in tragedy.

1980 A bomb attack during the Oktoberfest claims 12 lives.

1990 The reunification of Germany.

1992 World Economic Summit Meeting held in Munich. New airport opens. Over 400,000 people participate in Germany's first *Lichterkette* (candle vigils) in Munich.

2003 Munich celebrates 350 years of opera.

2006 Opening ceremony and match of the soccer World Cup in Munich.

2008 Munich celebrates its 850th birthday.

2014 As Munich signed up to become a European hydrogen fuel hub, BMW unveiled their H2R Hydrogen car.

Index

Munich 25 Best

WRITTEN BY Teresa Fisher
UPDATED BY Christopher and Melanie Rice
SERIES EDITOR Clare Ashton
COVER DESIGN Chie Ushio, Yuko Inagaki
DESIGN WORK Tracey Freestone
IMAGE RETOUCHING AND REPRO Jacqueline Street-Elkayam

Published in the United Kingdom by AA Publishing

ISBN 978-1-1018-7932-0

SIXTH EDITION

Color separation by AA Digital Department
Printed and bound by Leo Paper Products, China

10 9 8 7 6 5 4 3 2 1

A05260
Maps in this title produced from mapping © MAIRDUMONT / Falk Verlag 2014 and data from openstreetmap.org © OpenStreetMap contributors
Transport map © Communicarta Ltd, UK

The Automobile Association would like to thank the following photographers, companies and picture libraries for their assistance in the preparation of this book.

2-18t AA/T Souter; **4tl** CL Schmitt/Munich Tourist Office; **5** R Sterflinger/Munich Tourist Office; **6cl** AA/C Sawyer; **6c** AA/T Souter; **6cr** L Kaster/Munich Tourist Office; **6bl** R Hetz/Munich Tourist Office; **6bc** AA/T Souter; **6br** BBMC Tobias Ranzinger; **7cl** AA/M Jourdan; **7c** AA/M Jourdan; **7cr** AA/M Jourdan; **7bl** J Wildgruber/Munich Tourist Office; **7bc** AA/M Jourdan; **7br** AA Photodisc; **10tr** AA/T Souter; **10/11c** B Römmelt/Munich Tourist Office; **10/11b** AA/C Sawyer; **11tl** AA/M Jourdan; **13tl** C Reiter/Munich Tourist Office; **13cl** AA/T Souter; **13bl** AA/T Souter; **14tr** AA/M Jourdan; **14cr** AA/C Sawyer; **14bcr** Bavaria Tourism; **14br** AA/M Jourdan; **16tr** C Reiter/Munich Tourist Office; **16tcr** Bavaria Filmstadt; **16cr** AA/J Holmes; **16br** AA/M Jourdan; **17tl** AA DigitalVision; **17tcl** BBMC Tobias Ranzinger; **17cl** AA/M Jourdan; **17bl** B Römmelt/Munich Tourist Office; **18tr** AA/C Sawyer; **18tcr** AA/T Souter; **18cr** Photodisc; **18br** A Müller/Munich Tourist Office; **19tl** AA/C Sawyer; **19tcl** U Romeis/Munich Tourist Office; **19cl** H Schmied/Munich Tourist Office; **19bcl** H Gebhardt/Munich Tourist Office; **19bl** AA/T Souter; **20/21** C Reiter/Munich Tourist Office; **24l** AA/M Jourdan; **24tr** T Krüger/Munich Tourist Office; **24br** AA/M Jourdan; **25t** AA/M Jourdan; **25bl** AA/C Sawyer; **25br** AA/C Sawyer; **26tl** AA/T Souter; **26tr** AA/T Souter; **27tl** A Müller/Munich Tourist Office; **27c** AA/C Sawyer; **27tr** A Müller/Munich Tourist Office; **28l** H Gebhardt/Munich Tourist Office; **28/29t** A Müller/Munich Tourist Office; **28/29b** B Römmelt/Munich Tourist Office; **28bc** S Böttcher/Munich Tourist Office; **29t** H Gebhardt/Munich Tourist Office; **29br** F Witzig/Munich Tourist Office; **29bc** B Römmelt/Munich Tourist Office; **30tl** AA/T Souter; **30tr** AA/T Souter; **31tl** A Müller/Munich Tourist Office; **31tr** A Müller/Munich Tourist Office; **32tl** PRISMA ARCHIVO/Alamy; **32tr** allOver images/ Alamy; **33tl** B Römmelt/Munich Tourist Office; **33tr** C Reiter/Munich Tourist Office; **34-35t** AA/M Jourdan; **34bl** AA/C Sawyer; **34br** C Reiter/Munich Tourist Office; **35** A Müller/Munich Tourist Office; **36** T Krieger/Munich Tourist Office; **37t** AA/T Souter; **38t** Photodisc; **39t** AA/C Sawyer; **40t** Digitalvision; **41t** AA/M Jourdan; **42t** AA/C Sawyer; **43** J Wildgruber/Munich Tourist Office; **46tl** Bayerisches Nationalmuseum; **46tc** Bayerisches Nationalmuseum; **46tr** Bayerisches Nationalmuseum; **47tl** AA/T Souter; **47tr** BBMC Tobias Ranzinger; **48tl** W Hösl/Munich Tourist Office; **48tr** U Romeis/Munich Tourist Office; **49tl** B Römmelt/Munich Tourist Office; **49tr** C Reiter/Munich Tourist Office; **50l** W Hösl/Munich Tourist Office; **50tr** AA/T Souter; **50br** F Mader/Munich Tourist Office; **51t** J Lutz/Munich Tourist Office; **51cl** AA/T Souter; **51cr** AA/M Jourdan; **52-53t** AA/M Jourdan; **52bl** W Hösl/Munich Tourist Office; **52br** AA/C Sawyer; **53b** T Krüger/Munich Tourist Office; **54t** AA/T Souter; **55t** AA/M Chaplow; **56t** Photodisc; **57t** W Hösl/Munich Tourist Office; **58t** AA/C Sawyer; **59** J Wildgruber/Munich Tourist Office; **62** © Roy Langstaff / Alamy; **63tl** W Hösl/Munich Tourist Office; **63tr** AA/C Sawyer; **64l** P Scarlandis/Munich Tourist Office; **64tr** H Schmied/Munich Tourist Office; **64c** AA/M Jourdan; **65t** M Prugger/Munich Tourist Office; **65cl** AA/T Souter; **65cr** AA/M Jourdan; **66t** U Romeis/Munich Tourist Office; **66cl** AA/T Souter; **66cr** A Müller/Munich Tourist Office; **67tl** J Wildgruber/Munich Tourist Office; **67cl** AA/T Souter; **67r** AA/T Souter; **68tl** C L Schmitt/Munich Tourist Office; **68tr** AA/C Sawyer; **69tl** J Sauer/Munich Tourist Office; **69tr** J Sauer/Munich Tourist Office; **70l** G Blank/Munich Tourist Office; **70tr** B Römmelt/Munich Tourist Office; **70cr** AA/M Jourdan; **71t** G Blank/Munich Tourist Office; **71cl** AA/M Jourdan; **71cr** AA/M Jourdan; **72t** AA/M Jourdan; **72bl** C Reiter/Munich Tourist Office; **72br** AA/C Sawyer; **73** AA/T Souter; **74t** Photodisc; **75** AA/T Souter; **76t** Brand X Pics; **77t** AA/M Jourdan; **78** AA/M Jourdan; **79** H Gebhardt/Munich Tourist Office; **82l** J Wildgruber/Munich Tourist Office; **82tr** Ruggiero/Munich Tourist Office; **82cr** Olympiapark München; **83t** H Gebhardt/Munich Tourist Office; **83c** Olympiapark München; **84tl** AA/M Jourdan; **84tr** B Römmelt/Munich Tourist Office; **84cl** AA/M Jourdan; **84cr** AA/C Sawyer; **85** C Reiter/Munich Tourist Office; **86tl** BMW Pictures; **86tr** BMW Pictures; **87-88t** AA/M Jourdan; **87bl** B Römmelt/Munich Tourist Office; **87br** B Römmelt/Munich Tourist Office; **88bl** AA/T Souter; **88br** R Hetz/Munich Tourist Office; **89t** AA/T Souter; **90t** AA/T Souter; **91t** AA/T Souter; **92t** AA/M Jourdan; **93** Bavaria Tourism; **96l** Bavaria Filmstadt; **96tr** Bavaria Filmstadt; **96cr** Bavaria Filmstadt; **97t** Bavaria Filmstadt; **97cl** Bavaria Filmstadt; **97cr** Bavaria Filmstadt; **98l** Bavaria Tourism; **98/99t** Bavaria Tourism; **98cl** Bavaria Tourism; **98c** Bavaria Tourism; **98/99** Bavaria Tourism; **99** Bavaria Tourism; **100tl** AA/T Souter; **100tr** J Wildgruber/Munich Tourist Office; **101-102t** AA/M Jourdan; **101bl** Allianz Arena; **101br** AA/A Baker; **102b** imagebroker/Alamy; **103t-106t** Bavaria Tourism; **103b** AA/A Baker; **103c** AA/T Souter; **103r** Bavaria Tourism; **104** AA/A Baker; **105bl** Bavaria Tourism; **105bc** AA/T Souter; **105br** Bavaria Tourism; **106bl** AA/T Souter; **106br** AA/T Souter; **107** AA/M Jourdan; **108-112t** AA/C Sawyer; **108tr** Photodisc; **108cr** Stockbyte; **108bcr** AA/M Jourdan; **108br** AA/M Jourdan; **113** AA/T Souter; **114-125t** J Sauer/Munich Tourist Office; **117b** AA/T Souter; **122** AA/T Souter; **124bl** AA/C Sawyer; **124bc** AA/T Souter; **124br** AA/T Souter; **125bl** AA/T Souter; **125br** AA/C Sawyer

Every effort has been made to trace the copyright holders, and we apologize in advance for any accidental errors. We would be happy to apply the corrections in the following edition of this publication.

TITLES IN THE SERIES